CREDIT FIX POWER

A Lawyer Reveals the Secrets to Exercising Your Credit Rights Under the Law...and Making Violators Pay

Craig K. Perry, Esq.

ISBN-13: 978-1-7329249-0-1 eBook edition

ISBN-13: 978-1-7329249-1-8 Paperback edition

Published by CFP Publishing
3450 W. Cheyenne Ave., Suite 400
North Las Vegas, Nevada 89032

Perry, Craig K., author
Credit Fix Power

Visit creditfixpower.com

Table of Contents

A NOTE ON WHY THIS BOOK IS DIFFERENT

If you're tired of trying to clean up your credit without success, if you've tried everything else, and nothing has worked, then this book if for you. If the fight to fix your credit reports is a war, then this book contains your rules of engagement, coupled with a strategy on how to win the war if you're tired of fighting losing battles. It's about a strategy of winning WHEN ALL ELSE FAILS.

If this happens to be your first time picking up a book on credit repair, congratulations! You're not going to waste any time losing; you're going to learn how to do things the right way *from the beginning*, by knowing the rules, building and executing your plans, and then unleashing an offensive attack to destroy your enemies when they cross the line. The good news is that the weapons of war you need to defeat the bad guys are contained in the consumer protection laws that already exist. The labels "bad guys" and "enemies" refer to the people who break the law and violate your rights.

With so many books on the market about credit repair, and tons of free information on the Internet, why should you own or read this book? The answer is because it is different from every other book you will find on the market, in several ways. It's the first book that was written by an attorney *for the consumer*. A few books written by lawyers about credit law exist, but they are written *for other lawyers*, and are too technical for most people who don't have experience in this area of the law to understand and implement. And even if you can get past the legal jargon, these books are expensive. "A lawyer's time is his stock in trade," said Abraham Lincoln. Since writing these technical legal books is time-consuming, and lawyers sell fewer copies to a small niche of readers, they charge more. For example, the National Consumer Law Center (NCLC.org) developed a two-volume set on the Fair Credit Reporting Act for lawyers that costs over $160, with updates running $160 *per year*, which includes the online and printed version. This book is inexpensive by comparison!

* * *

This book contains many explanations and how-to instructions for do-it-yourself consumers. In addition to this book, I offer consumers other services; some may want to take advantage of them. Some services are free, because when violators break the law, they are required to pay attorneys' fees and costs—not you. These additional services are discussed in Chapter 2, Chapter 15, or you go can to CreditFixPower.com for more information.

In the first paragraph, I gave you two reasons why this book is different. Here are three additional reasons why this book is different from all the others:

3. Other books about consumer credit reporting rarely refer to the actual laws that they are explaining. This book refers repeatedly to that body of law that makes fixing your credit possible, namely the *Fair Credit Reporting Act*! In a nutshell, the Fair Credit Reporting Act (FCRA) is the group of federal laws that applies to issues surrounding your consumer files, credit and consumer reports, your credit profile, and credit score. In this book, I provide Internet links where you can go and read these statutes for yourself. So, if you are reading the print version of this book, you'll want to have an Internet-connected device nearby, so you can look up these statutes online at the law.cornell.edu website, which is the best website I have found and a super-easy way to navigate this law, as I will demonstrate later.

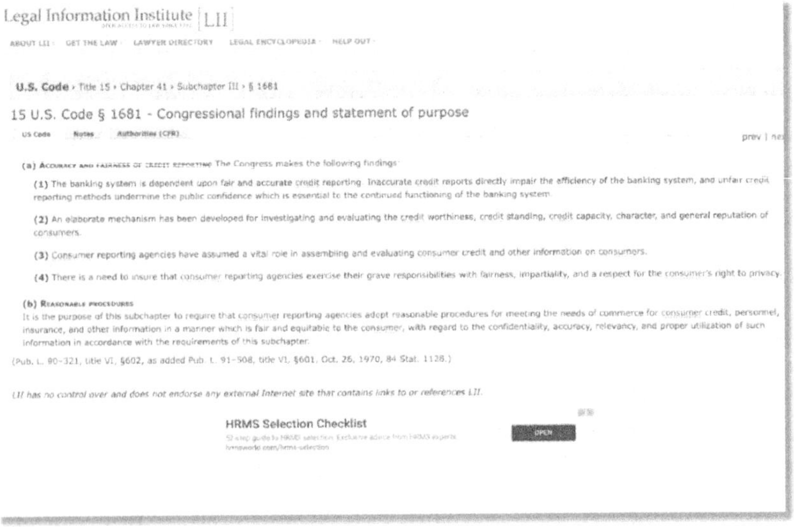

Legal Information Institute [LII]

ABOUT LII · GET THE LAW · LAWYER DIRECTORY · LEGAL ENCYCLOPEDIA · HELP OUT

U.S. Code › Title 15 › Chapter 41 › Subchapter III › § 1681

15 U.S. Code § 1681 - Congressional findings and statement of purpose

US Code | Notes | Authorities (CFR)

prev | ne

(a) Accuracy and fairness of credit reporting The Congress makes the following findings:

(1) The banking system is dependent upon fair and accurate credit reporting. Inaccurate credit reports directly impair the efficiency of the banking system, and unfair credit reporting methods undermine the public confidence which is essential to the continued functioning of the banking system.

(2) An elaborate mechanism has been developed for investigating and evaluating the credit worthiness, credit standing, credit capacity, character, and general reputation of consumers.

(3) Consumer reporting agencies have assumed a vital role in assembling and evaluating consumer credit and other information on consumers.

(4) There is a need to insure that consumer reporting agencies exercise their grave responsibilities with fairness, impartiality, and a respect for the consumer's right to privacy.

(b) Reasonable procedures

It is the purpose of this subchapter to require that consumer reporting agencies adopt reasonable procedures for meeting the needs of commerce for consumer credit, personnel, insurance, and other information in a manner which is fair and equitable to the consumer, with regard to the confidentiality, accuracy, relevancy, and proper utilization of such information in accordance with the requirements of this subchapter.

(Pub. L. 90-321, title VI, §602, as added Pub. L. 91-508, title VI, §601, Oct. 26, 1970, 84 Stat. 1128.)

LII has no control over and does not endorse any external Internet site that contains links to or references LII.

HRMS Selection Checklist

4. Another feature that makes this book unique is its broad scope. All other consumer books that deal with your credit only focus on how to improve your credit score. However, there is so much more to the Fair Credit Reporting Act (FCRA) that you should

know! The FCRA empowers you to (1) find out literally *everything* about you that is in their files that could be shared with someone else (i.e., more than what is on your credit report), (2) find out what they actually did to investigate your disputes, (3) learn who is accessing your credit files and why, and (4) place credit alerts or freezes on your credit report.

5. The final reason why this book is unique is because it navigates you through the complexities of the FCRA and along the pathway of enforcement such that you can exercise your *ultimate right* under the FCRA: the right to *sue violators*. Not only will you be able to sue when necessary when you comply with these laws, but also law firms like mine can represent you to force compliance or make them pay for the damages you incur.

* * *

In short, you are the ideal reader for this book if you (1) want to avoid mistakes the first time you write your letters or (2) have sent letters repeatedly without a proper response. You've probably heard the sad-but-true definition of *insanity*: doing the *same thing* over and over again, expecting a *different* result. Some consumers write the same dispute letters repeatedly, expecting a correction or deletion to magically occur. All the credit repair materials that I have read recommend—that if at first you don't succeed, try, try again. I understand the impulse, because I used to do the same thing for my clients many years ago, writing letters over and over again to deaf credit bureaus, before I truly grasped the power of the FCRA. Today, I don't waste my time begging known violators with never-ending letter campaigns to comply with the law; *nothing gets their attention faster than a lawsuit.* It's sad but true, and it's a weapon in your arsenal that—although it should be used judiciously—it should be used whenever necessary. It's why I entitled this book CREDIT FIX POWER!

Do I recommend that you sue a violator without representation? You can, but I wouldn't recommend that for two reasons. First, the learning curve is steep. You must learn legal procedures for filing, serving, and prosecuting a case. A consumer law attorney can properly screen your case, file suit, prosecute the case, and make violators pay, often without any up-front attorneys' fees or costs paid by you. The FCRA requires that violators pay your reasonable attorney's fees and costs. When Congress passed the FCRA, they felt so strongly about ensuring that consumers receive protection under this law that they provided for your right to sue and mandated that violators would pay your attorneys' fees and costs. For those reasons, hiring an attorney to prosecute violators is worth your consideration.

* * *

To summarize, here's why this book is different from all of the other consumer credit reporting books and why you should own it, read it, and use it:

It's written by an experienced credit law attorney who knows the law and has reduced it down in very simple language for the non-technical consumer;

- It's an inexpensive book, putting it within the grasp of every consumer who is serious about understanding credit reporting laws;
- It does more than provide general information; it provides statutory references each time a point of law is discussed

and shows how to properly communicate with suppliers, aggregators, and users of information about you;

- It covers all the essential aspects of the FCRA, not simply a narrow portion of the statute;
- It recognizes that despite your *best efforts*, you will still have persons and entities who violate the provisions of the FCRA. This book shows you how to properly exercise your rights so that you have the option of hiring a competent lawyer to enforce those rights that all too often are violated.

The one thing that this book does not cover extensively are the voluminous number of legal opinions from state and federal courts that continually interpret this statute. Case law developed by the courts is beyond the scope of this book—there are thousands of cases that deal with the FCRA. Currently, the FCRA is receiving a lot of attention, and more opinions are expected to emerge that will continue to provide guidance about the application of this statute in a variety of situations.

* * *

DISCLAIMER: *This book is for educational purposes only. I am not your attorney, and this book does not create an attorney-client relationship. If you want legal advice that specifically addresses your unique concerns, retain counsel. Also, these laws, and how they are understood or interpreted, change over time. Although future editions and updates are planned to reflect major changes and interpretations, changes may occur before the next edition is released. Court rulings and administrative decisions usually develop gradually over time, but with the increased attention this law is receiving, changes and interpretations are expected to come with greater frequency.*

INTRODUCTION

Have you ever been denied credit? Have you ever paid higher interest rates than preferred borrowers? Have you ever paid higher-than-normal insurance premiums or been denied coverage? Have you ever been denied employment after a "background check?" Finally, have you ever been denied credit even though you have a good credit score?

Many of these types of decisions are governed by what shows up on your consumer report or your credit score. But what happens if errors are found on these reports that are partly to blame for low scores, denials of credit, high rates, and lost job opportunities? Each year, millions of Americans report that they have found errors on their credit reports.

The generators of these consumer reports, these Consumer Reporting Agencies (CRAs), sell information *about* you that you never see, stuff that does *not* show up on the credit reports that you order. CRAs have more information to sell to potential users than you ever imagined; the information that they sell, known and unknown, can dramatically affect your access to lines of credit, low interest rates, employment, and insurance—to name just a few. This information also affects rental opportunities, access to utilities and banking, and the amounts that you pay for goods and services.

CRAs gather and sell any information they are permitted—sometimes even more. They can share your information with any legally permissible user, for a price. Sometimes they're caught crossing the line, selling information illegally or to unqualified users, or without following proper procedures to ensure maximum accuracy, as required by a law that you will soon get to know, the Fair Credit Reporting Act (FCRA).

(Note: laws of the United States passed by Congress and signed into law by the President are organized into a body of law called the "United States Code" or "U.S. Code," which is usually abbreviated as "U.S.C." The FCRA is codified as 15 U.S.C. § 1681 et seq. "15" is one of the "Titles" of the U.S. Code. "§" is the symbol for "section." The FCRA begins with section 1681a and ends with section 1681x. "Et seq." is Latin for "and what follows." So, the proper way to reference this law is 15 U.S.C. § 1681 et seq. The best place to read the FCRA is at the law website for Cornell University.)

* * *

Day after day, year after year, the files that CRAs maintain about consumers increase in size and scope. For them, selling data about you to others is big business, generating billions of dollars in profits.

The FCRA is a federal statute that makes it very clear what may be collected and sold to users about you. Unfortunately, the breadth of the definition regarding what CRAs can collect and sell is staggering.

Look at the broad definition provided in the FCRA. "Consumer reports" (notice the statute uses the broader term *consumer*, not *credit*) can contain "any written, oral, or other communication of *any information* by a consumer reporting agency bearing on a consumer's credit worthiness, credit standing, credit capacity, *character*, *general reputation*, *personal characteristics*, or *mode of living*" that could play a factor in your access to credit, insurance or employment. See 15 U.S.C. § 1681a(d)(1). With certain restrictions, such information can come from neighbors, friends, and other persons with whom you may be acquainted. See 15 U.S.C. § 1681a(e). If it can come from these sources, can't they also collect information from things you and others post on social media such as Facebook, Twitter, Instagram, and YouTube? At most, they have to follow "reasonable procedures" to corroborate the information from an additional source or demonstrate that "the person interviewed is the best possible source of the information." See 15 U.S.C. § 1681d(4)(A) and (B).

15 U.S.C. § 1681m speaks about information about you that could be obtained from third persons, not just CRAs, regarding your

"credit worthiness, credit standing, credit capacity, character, general reputation, personal characteristics, or mode of living."

In other words, the scope and sources from which CRAs can collect information about you is so broad that CRAs can collect, store and report just about any information they can get their hands on. After all, what piece of information could not (arguably) influence the users who make decisions about you, whether to hire you, loan your money, or sell you insurance?

* * *

The potential for error and abuse is not theoretical—it's real. Let's talk about a case that went to court back in the 1970s after the FCRA was passed—and light-years before modern tools of information-gathering and dissemination via the Internet and social media were available.

In 1971, Mr. James Millstone applied for auto insurance. His insurance agent procured him a policy with an insurance company named Firemen's Fund Insurance Company, but the policy was canceled the day after it took effect.

Naturally, Mr. Millstone was perplexed, and he wanted to know why it was canceled so abruptly and unexpectedly. At the time, Millstone was working as the news editor for a local newspaper. He knew how to investigate. Millstone learned that the cancellation was the result of a credit report provided by O'Hanlon Reports, Inc. Millstone demanded to know what was in that report that would cause a cancellation. Was it because he had a bad credit score? He couldn't think of one good reason.

When Millstone finally got his hands on the credit report, he was shocked! The report said the following: "The file shows that you are very much disliked by your neighbors at that location and were considered to be a 'hippy type'...."

Was he really denied because his neighbors reported he was, among other things, a "hippy type?" Yes, but there was more. He read on:

"[Y]ou participated in many demonstrations in Washington, D.C....The file shows that you were strongly suspected of being a drug user by neighbors, but they could not positively substantiate these suspicions. You're shown to have shoulder-length hair and a beard [and] there were rumors in the neighborhood that you have been evicted from three previous residences."

Because of this report, based purely upon rumor and conjecture, Millstone's character was maligned, and the information placed on a credit report. On this basis alone, not because of a credit score or borrowing history, the insurance company summarily canceled his auto insurance policy.

Millstone sought justice, suing the consumer reporting agency, O'Hanlon reports. At trial, Millstone received an award, in today's dollars (2018), $11,700 in actual damages, and $117,000 in punitive damages. The defendant appealed the award, but the decision was upheld. For more information, look up *Millstone v. O'Hanlon Reports, Inc.*, 383 F. Supp. 269 (E.D. Mo. 1974) by clicking here, Millstone Case, or go to Appendix 1 of this book to read the opinion in its entirety. This is not an isolated case; many more examples could be cited.

As an attorney who practices in the area of consumer protection, I wrote this book to help you see the type of information that is being gathered and disseminated about you, and the harm that information can do when it is erroneous, stolen, or sold to the wrong people.

Some of the information that lands on your credit report shouldn't be there: wrong names, inaccurate information, etc.

The more sinister side of the CRAs is the information that doesn't show up on your *credit* report but does show up on a *consumer* report that you never see, unless you pursue it with dogged determination.

Like Mr. Millstone did.

Again, why does this stuff matter so much? Because making sure that CRAs maintain accurate consumer files and credit reports can dramatically affect your quality of life.

Accurate information gathered by CRAs, such as Equifax, Experian, and Trans Union can help you (a) qualify for needed loans, (b) get the best possible interest rates, (c) save thousands of dollars in loan situations, and (d) help you get the capital you need for investments, purchases, or other opportunities.

Even if you are already aware of these possible problems, maybe you don't know exactly how to use the law to improve your own situation.

This book is also for you.

* * *

Before you act on the information in this book, follow this tip:

Read the entire book before you start taking action! You won't gain an understanding about all aspects of the law until you read the entire book. Better letters mean better results, and more legal grounds to enforce your rights.

You may have bought this book because you are either having credit problems or credit score issues. Or maybe you bought this book to figure out if there's any way to legally enforce your rights. This book can help you fix your credit the *right* way, with maximum legal power. Instead of being ignored, you will get results!

* * *

Perhaps your score is good, but you're still being denied credit. This book will reveal the secrets why that is the case, and how you can uncover that information.

As a consumer, you have the right to expect that the information in your consumer file (1) belongs to you, (2) is accurate, and (3) is verifiable.

You've probably heard it said, "If you don't *know* your rights, you don't *have any*." This is especially true when it comes to information stored by others about you and your credit-worthiness. Most people have no idea what their rights are or how to enforce them.

My law practice is committed to helping consumers like you, across the country, prosecute those who violate the laws and force them to take corrective action.

It is my hope that you will come to appreciate the Fair Credit Reporting Act and learn how to use it to provide you with better credit and protection of your identity and personal information.

CHAPTER 1: LOCKED OUT

Without good credit, modern life becomes difficult. Even if you're not planning to buy a home or even a car, bad credit follows you. Do you have to buy car insurance? Co-sign on your child's loan? Need homeowner's insurance? Use credit cards? Own a business? The interest rates and premiums you pay are all tied to your *credit risk*, or how sellers of goods, services, insurance, and loans perceive your ability to pay or repay.

It's not just about your credit or your credit score, either. CRAs are collecting a lot more information about you than you could ever imagine. If they would give you a full disclosure of your consumer file (discussed in a later chapter), you'd understand the full extent to which these companies are gathering information about you.

Being able to get the things in life that you want, including your employment opportunities, is tied to what information CRAs and other institutions are gleaning, compiling, aggregating and selling to the decision makers (the "users" or "buyers"). Once the information becomes digitized, it can be made available to anyone—for a price. Trusted institutions lacking in adequate protection are allowing sensitive information about you drain away like water through a sieve.

Yes, the information that is being gathered about you would shock you. Consumer reporting agencies are not called *credit* reporting agencies because they collect more than that kind of information about you.

Think about Millstone. If they could have this kind of information on someone in 1971, think what kind of information they could have on you with today's technology! This is why I'll show you in a subsequent chapter how to request a copy of your complete *consumer* (not *credit*) file.

You probably thought that all of this talk about fixing your credit was simply about your credit *score*. It's not. Those of you who know a little more might think it's all about your credit *profile*, a broader term. Again, this is only part of the picture. What companies want now is your complete *consumer profile*—who you are, what you look like, what zip code you came from, where your parents lived, and how much is in your bank account or savings right now, as well as the amount of your recent paychecks and deposits. And they can get all of this information without even asking your permission; they simply buy it from data aggregators.

Sellers of goods and services want to know where you are all the time. Google's motto is a laughable "do no evil," as it gathers information about your whereabouts even when you turn off its location services on your mobile phone.[i]

Facebook tracks your every online movement, delivering spot-on ads tailored to suit your potential interests.[ii] Eye-tracking software, keyword searches and software "cookies" complete the picture. And of course, to top it off, the National Security Agency (NSA) has software installed on every ISP server in the country, recording emails, phone calls and your movement.[iii] The NSA even turns on microphones and cameras on your mobile phone—even when they appear to be turned off.[iv]

* * *

Although this book is not going to address all these matters, it will do three things. (1) It will help you to find out what is in your entire consumer file compiled by each CRA, (2) it will assist you in following the proper legal steps to remove erroneous and unverifiable information from your credit report—or you can make violators pay—and (3) it will teach you the steps to block some of the information that is being shared with others. If you follow these steps, and still you are ignored by the CRAs, by persons who provide erroneous information to the CRAs, and users who pull your credit reports without a permissible purpose, you will have legal cause to initiate litigation and sue these violators, as provided in the FCRA.

Without good credit, you are locked out of a better life, spending tens if not hundreds of thousands of dollars over your lifetime on interest that you could have put towards retirement, savings, and a better quality of life.

You can already find several books on the market explaining what you need to do to improve your credit score. If you join CreditKarma.com, you can see what elements go into making up your credit score, such as whether you maintain lower credit card balances, age of existing credit, your recent application for new credit, the making of timely payments, etc.

This book drills deep the statutory tools available to improve your credit: how to correctly request fixing errors that appear on your report, how to find out undisclosed information you don't know about that you with lenders and other users, how to freeze your credit, and how to put yourself in a position to prosecute violators, as a *last resort*, when they ignore you and fail to take proper action as required by law.

Thousands of lawsuits are filed annually against violators of the FCRA, which is some indication that violations are commonplace; in fact, lawsuits represent a tiny fraction of the violations that occur. It's critical that you learn how to use the protections guaranteed by the FCRA. If you fail to follow the steps outlined by the FCRA, you or your attorney will not be able to successfully sue violators.

* * *

The next few chapters will teach (a) how to properly comply with the requirements of the law, (b) how to spot violators of the law, and (c) how to help you preserve evidence in support of your claim, should you decide that legal action is your only remaining recourse to ensure credit report accuracy and transparency, as to the information that CRAs maintain about you.

CHAPTER 2: MORE HELP IS ON THE WAY

This book is designed for consumers who want to become more informed about their rights in the area of credit reporting laws and what they can do when violations occur. In order to meet the needs of consumers with different needs, talents and time, I provide three options:

Option 1: Power Tools. Since you have already purchased the book, you can receive free downloads (basic form letters, contact info of 55 separate credit reporting agencies) by signing up for a free membership at CreditFixPower.com;

Option 2: Power Toolbox. Gain access to over 50 downloadable sample letters to use with consumer reporting agencies; and

Option 3: Attorney Power Package. In addition to this book, free Power Tools, and the Power Toolbox, our law firm will review your credit reports, looking for errors, and write dispute letters to the CRAs.

For greater details and additional help about available options, go to Chapter 15, or visit CreditFixPower.com.

CHAPTER 3: FILES AND REPORTS: GETTING THE DEFINITIONS RIGHT

Throughout this book, I'm going to use four terms that you need to keep straight:

1. Consumer Files;
2. Credit Files;
3. Consumer Reports; and
4. Credit Reports.

These terms are not interchangeable. I'll explain the differences and illustrate those differences in two figures.

A. **The Consumer File**. The consumer file, in its broadest definition, is "all of the information" held by any consumer agency about you. See 15 U.S.C. § 1681g. CRAs are permitted to collect "*any* written, oral, or other communication of *any information* by a consumer reporting agency bearing on a consumer's credit worthiness, credit standing, credit capacity, character, general reputation, personal characteristics, or mode of living" that could play a factor in your access to credit, insurance, or employment. 15 U.S.C. § 1681a(d)(1) (Italics added for emphasis).

In a nutshell, "CRAs provide data that is used by issuers of credit or insurance, or by employers, landlords, and others in making eligibility decisions affecting consumers." Read https://www.privacyrights.org/blog/tutorial-data-brokers-and-people-search-sites.

This is a very broad definition, indeed. Here are some examples about what CRAs can (and do) collect about you—the list will surprise you:

A. Your credit history with banks, which includes credit cards;

B. Your history of paying your bills with other creditors, including medical providers and utility companies;

C. Your landlord-tenant rental payment history;

D. Current and past bank account balances;

E. The amount of your paychecks (sold to CRAs by payroll processing companies like ADP);

F. Your criminal record;

G. Any public record from any court records or county recorder's office;

H. Your property ownership history;

I. Your past and present addresses;

J. Your name and any aliases;

K. Your age (date of birth), marital status, and number of children and their ages;

L. Your marital history (divorces, etc.);

M. Your level of education;

N. Whether you have children in college;

O. Who you might be related to;

P. The affluence of the area in which you live, or your parents live (or lived) as determined by zip code;

Q. Your political party affiliation (voting records);

R. Your home and mobile phone number(s);

S. Your employment history;

T. Information reported by or gathered from past or present neighbors;

U. Any information you publish publicly, or opinions expressed publicly;

V. Pictures and comments made on social media platforms such as Facebook and Twitter;

W. Information taken from any of your websites; and

X. Anything else CRAs can get their hands on or purchase from data brokers fitting within the broad definition of 15 U.S.C. § 1681a(d)(1).

Are you beginning to see what can be filed away in your *consumer* file? It's much broader that what any one credit report might contain.

B. **The Credit File**. CRAs and their attorneys try to conflate ("merge" the meanings of) the terms "consumer files" with "credit files." Even courts sometimes seem to use these terms interchangeably, but they are not synonymous. Just look at what types of reports you can buy from CRAs. It's a much broader array of choices than the term *credit file* would lead you to believe; it can contain any or all of the items listed above. The credit file is a subset of the consumer file—it is not the same.

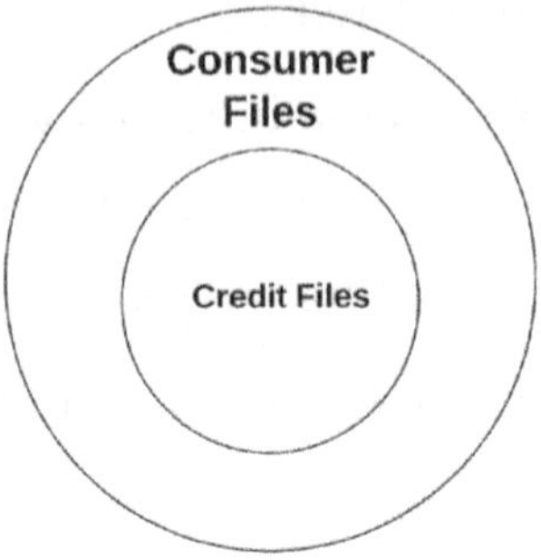

Remember this statement: *All credit files are consumer files, but not all consumer files are credit files.* As you can see from the figure above, a credit file is part of the consumer file. Next, out of the consumer

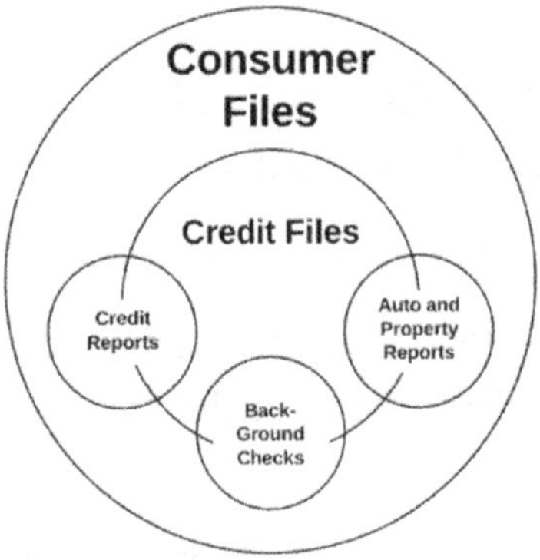

file come various types of consumer reports; credit reports are only one type of report that CRAs can generate from a consumer file:

C. **Credit Reports**. Credit reports are compilations of data from your consumer files that deal with credit issues that may be of interest to buyers who will use this information to evaluate you.

D. **Consumer Reports**. Consumer reports include Credit Reports and every other type of information sold by the CRAs to users, but do not contain a person's criminal history. This is proof that there is more information they store than they give to consumers. Such information is sold in other types of *consumer* reports. "Background checks" are a form of *consumer* reports, information aggregated by CRAs and sold to employers or to the government. You should be starting to see that there's a difference between a *credit* report and a *consumer* report.

In summary, your consumer file contains all of the information aggregated by a consumer reporting agency about you—everything. A credit file is part (subset) of a consumer file. From a consumer file, CRAs generate consumer reports. Some of those consumer reports are credit reports, but there many kinds of consumer reports that can be generated from your consumer file. It just depends upon what type of data a particular CRA is collecting about you and selling to others.

Keeping these terms straight is important to understanding the chapters that follow. For example, a later chapter will show you how to request a *full file disclosure.*

CHAPTER 4: THE KEY TO FIXING REPORTING ERRORS

This is the most important chapter in this book. It sets forth seven essential consumer rights embodied in the Fair Credit Reporting Act. It also provides an understanding of what you can do when those rights have been overlooked, ignored, or willfully trampled by violators.

This book does *not* address many of the basic, obvious things that many books discuss about how to improve your credit score by such things as lowering credit card balances, holding on to aged credit lines, not applying for new lines of credit, avoiding late pays, etc. Instead, this chapter and those that follow dig deep on one thing: how to use the Fair Credit Reporting Act to benefit your quality of life—today and in the future.

* * *

Consumer Reporting Agencies have been heavily regulated since 1970, and for good reason. Today in this Information Age, we need the FCRA more than ever!

Because of the free flow of information in our day, the amount of information that CRAs can collect, store and share about you is greater than ever before. This information is so valuable that criminals are constantly attempting to hack into it—and sometimes they are successful.

With the increase in data collection comes the plague of corrupted data and misreporting of data that can find its way into your consumer files and your consumer reports, which are then shared with users who make decisions that affect you, some examples of which you will read about below. Therefore, you must remain vigilant!

* * *

In a nutshell, here's the problem that needs to be prevented or fixed:

INFORMATION THAT IS STOLEN, OR FALSE INFORMATION THAT DOES NOT BELONG IN YOUR CONSUMER FILES AND CONSUMER REPORTS CAN DESTROY YOUR CREDIT SCORES—AND LEAD TO CANCELED CREDIT, NO CREDIT, HIGHER INTEREST RATES, LOSS OF JOB OPPORTUNITIES, NO INSURANCE, OR HIGHER INSURANCE PREMIUMS.

These are devastating consequences—and all it takes is for bad information to be added to and remain in your consumer files. Let me share with you real life examples from lawsuits that have been filed in court that *prove* the significant consequences caused by violators, and how much jurors dislike these violators.

Loss of employment opportunities. Kevin Mills applied for a position at Starbucks. He was hired, subject to the successful completion of a background investigation by a consumer reporting agency. The background check came back with two convictions for domestic violence. In fact, Kevin Mills had never been convicted of domestic violence. He received a call from Starbucks indicating that they would not be hiring him based upon the contents of the consumer report. Later, the report came in the mail telling him why he had not been hired. He contacted the consumer reporting agency who provided the information, disputed the information, and they realized that they had made a mistake. Even though the mistake was cleared up, Starbucks would not reconsider their decision not to hire him. *Kevin Wills v. Starbucks Corporation*, Active Case, No. 1:17-CV-03654-CAP-CMS. The case has been stayed pending further settlement negotiations as of the time of publication of this book.

Loss of Credit. A consumer contacted my office recently. She had accidentally made a partial payment on one of her credit card bills and was short a few dollars. The next month, her credit reports indicated that she had not made any payment. Two weeks later, two banks who had issued her other credit cards canceled their lines of credit.

Loss of Earning Capacity. One of my current clients went to use a credit card to rent a hotel room while working a job out of state. The hotel ran his card and told him it was declined. He called the bank and found out that they said he had recently filed bankruptcy; however, his bankruptcy had been filed more than 10 years before that, and he had dismissed the bankruptcy, after he had regained employment. He asked for the mistaken information to be removed, but he was ignored. Because of this, he was denied credit lines that would have allowed him to take on more work. He also had to pay two to three times the regular interest rate to purchase cars for his family members.

Cancellation of Insurance. Remember the Millstone case, cited in the first chapter of this book. Because his neighbors thought he was a "hippy type" and "possible" drug user, his auto insurance was canceled.

All of these problems could have been resolved applying the laws set forth in the Fair Credit Reporting Act. The FCRA is your key to correcting mistakes on your credit and other consumer reports that can deeply affect your life. The FCRA is also the tool you use to combat identity theft.

The FCRA can't fully benefit you if you don't know what your rights are, and what you must do to exercise them. You must *do* certain things or the FCRA does little to benefit you. For example, you need to write letters, complain, make your case, request information, etc. (For most people, the only way they use the FCRA is to obtain free copies of their credit reports each year.)

Your key to (a) maintaining accurate credit reports, (b) knowing what information each CRA has stored about you that goes into your consumer reports (some of which you generally never see), and (c) protecting your identity, is found in the Fair Credit Reporting Act.

In order to turn that key, you have to know *what* to do and *how* to do it. This is what the next few chapters will explain to you.

* * *

Know Your Rights!

Many consumer protection laws have been passed at both the federal and state levels. (See the Bonus Materials in Chapter 6 to gain a better understanding of other federal legislation that has been passed.)

In 2003, Congress passed the Fair Accounting and Transactions Act (FACTA), which was added to the FCRA. This provided further protection from identity theft and enacted measures that you can take in the event that your identity is stolen.

The FCRA contains several consumer rights. You must be proactive to exercise some of them. Here is a list of your important rights:

A List of Your Most Important Rights Under the FCRA

1. **Accuracy**. You have the right to expect that before reporting information about you, CRAs will "follow reasonable procedures to assure maximum possible accuracy of the information." See 15 U.S.C. § 1681e(b);

1. **Correcting Errors**. You have the right to request corrections and deletions to errors noted on your credit reports, consumer reports, and things someone *could see* that are contained in your consumer files; CRAs and furnishers must both conduct reasonable investigations. See 15 U.S.C. § 1681i and 15 U.S.C. § 1681s-2(b), respectively;
2. **Permissible Users**. You have the right to sue those who do not have a permissible purpose to obtain information from your consumer report. See 15 U.S.C. § 1681b;
3. **Identity Theft Protection**. You have the right to request a credit freeze or credit block to keep users from accessing your consumer files. See 15 U.S.C. § 1681c-1 and 15 U.S.C. § 1681c-2;
4. **Full File Disclosure**. You have the right to request a full disclosure of everything that is in your consumer files, and receive a copy of the same. See 15 U.S.C. § 1681g(a)(2); and

5. **Scope of Investigation**. You have the right to find out what a CRA did to investigate your request for correction or deletion. 15 U.S.C. § 1681i(a)(6)(B)(iii).

6. **The Right to Sue.** The FCRA grants you the right to sue a violator of the law. This right is discussed in detail in this book, and is a critical tool you must consider, when all else fails.

* * *

7 Important Credit Report Rights

1. Accuracy
2. Deletion and Correction of Errors and Unverifiable Info
3. Limited Access to Your Credit Info
4. Identify Theft Protection
5. Full Disclosure of Your Consumer Files
6. The Scope of a Reinvestigation
7. The Right to Sue Violators

Enforcing Your Rights

The chapters that follow will show you how you can exercise your rights under the FCRA. The remainder of this chapter will show you what you can do if you are overlooked, ignored, or willfully mistreated by a CRA, furnisher, or user who violates the statute.

Although it should be used with discretion, when all else fails, you may have to take violators to court.

Specifically, when a CRA fails to comply with the FCRA, the law grants consumers the right to sue the CRA, furnishers, or users who violate this statute. The law also permits a consumer's attorney to receive reasonable attorney's fees and costs from violator(s). Both of these provisions empower consumers to seek statutory, actual, and/or punitive damages from violators. To help you appreciate each of these provisions, a discussion follows.

* * *

The Right to Sue. One of the key features of many consumer protection laws, including the FCRA, is the right of the consumer to sue when a violation occurs. This is called the right to bring a "private right of action."

When the law permits a private right of action, the consumer, of themselves or through an attorney, can bring an action against a consumer reporting agency, furnisher, or user of the information who has violated the law.

It's important to remember that many state and federal laws do *not* always grant consumers the right to sue, or in other words, maintain a *private right of action.* Many consumer protection statutes only give governmental administrative agencies the authority to enforce the laws that legislators have passed. Sometimes, administrative agencies don't enforce the laws the way consumers think they could or should; decisions about law enforcement are made by the executive branch, and in some cases are made based upon the financial resources available to the government to enforce such laws; discussions on this topic alone could fill an entire book.

Laws like the FCRA, as well as the FDCPA (see Bonus Materials in this book), which give consumers the right to bring a private right of action, grant an exceptional and important privilege to consumers. A private right of action, in my opinion, makes it more likely that these laws will be enforced, because they empower consumers to take prompt action on a single violation when it occurs, without waiting for action by an overworked and poorly funded administrative agency which may never be able to get to their case, perhaps in the interests of more demanding or important cases.

* * *

Allowance for Attorneys' Fees and Costs, aka the "Fee Shifting" Provision of the FCRA. In addition to permitting to bring a private right of action, lawyers representing consumers do not have to ask their clients to pay the attorney's fees.

The FCRA requires violators to pay the reasonable fees and costs to attorneys representing consumer victims. Under the normal "American Rule" of paying attorneys' fees, each side normally bears their own fees and costs. A "fee-shifting" provision shifts the burden on the violator of the statute to pay the consumer's fees.

Because the statute requires violators to pay these fees, consumers should seriously consider retaining counsel to proceed with their case, rather than suing on their own behalf. Consumers who sue on their own behalf, are called *pro se* litigants, or litigants suing *in proper person,* and may not be granted attorney's fees, but probably the costs of the suit will be awarded if the consumer prevails.

Both the consumer's right to sue and the fee-shifting provisions of the FCRA increase the likelihood that violators will be prosecuted and be less likely to commit violations in the future.

* * *

The Correct Way to Exercise Your Rights

Let's look at the big picture for a moment. Some violations occur without you having to do anything—no letter writing campaign is needed—you only need to spot them. However, in order to spot them, you have to learn what to look for:

- CRAs that do not take steps to ensure maximum accuracy;
- CRAs that give your information to unapproved users;
- Users who request information without good cause; and
- CRAs who fail to protect your data from theft by hackers.

On the other hand, in order to exercise your other rights, you must *do* something first (i.e., exercise your rights), and if the CRAs and furnishers *do not respond correctly*, then they have violated your rights. Here are some examples of rights that you can exercise:

1. **Dispute Letter(s)**. If there is an error on your credit report, and you want it fixed, you must write letters to the CRAs asking them to investigate. They are also required to notify the furnisher of the information, who must also investigate. Both investigations must be *reasonable* and be completed within 30 to 45 days.
2. **Full File Disclosure Request(s)**. If you want to see all information in your consumer file, then you must request a copy in writing. If the CRAs don't provide it, then the CRA is in violation of the law.
3. **Freezing Your Credit**. If you are a victim of identity theft, you can freeze (i.e., block) access to your credit report. You have to contact the CRAs and provide required information,

which obligates them to freeze your credit. When done correctly, if the CRAs do not follow through on your request, they violate the law.

As you can see, each of these rights require you to take proper action. The next few chapters explain how to exercise your rights in the proper manner.

CHAPTER 5: THE DUTY TO VERIFY OR DELETE

The Consumer Financial Protection Bureau (CFPB), the FCC, and rulings from the bench have all made it clear that the purpose of the FCRA is to make sure consumer reports contain accurate *and* verifiable information. It cannot be one or the other; the information on a credit report must be *both.*

Put another way, if the information on your report is accurate but cannot be verified, it must be deleted from the report. This principle is important to understand, because in my experience, many of the furnishers who report debts are down-the-line debt buyers (also called "junk-debt buyers") who do not have any original account level documentation, nor can they access them according to the terms of the contract that they sign with either predecessor debt buyers or original creditors. In other words, debt buyers who furnish much of what goes onto credit reports cannot verify the debt they are reporting, and by contract are not allowed to request that information, even if it did exist.

* * *

First, let me explain more about the reasons why I believe many debt collectors cannot verify the debts they are reporting. Imagine that a creditor, such as a mobile phone company, extends credit to a consumer. The consumer allegedly does not pay her or his bill, and the bill goes into collection. The first debt collector tries for 90 days to encourage the consumer to pay. If unsuccessful, the debt is sold to another debt collector, who is also a debt *buyer.* The debt buyer pays 6 cents for every dollar of uncollectible debt that it buys. Let's say the phone bill is $1,000.00, so the debt buyer purchases the debt for $60.00. The phone company writes off the loss as bad debt against their income. This happens multiple times to the phone company. They don't typically sell one bad account to a debt buyer; they sell dozens, hundreds, or thousands at a time. One bill of sale is prepared, and the debt buyer purchases a whole batch of bad debt for 6 cents on the dollar.

Do you think that the creditor wants to spend its time and energy helping the debt collector get paid in full for all of this bad debt it had to write off? Certainly not. To avoid getting pulled into using its time and resources helping the debt collector make huge sums of money on this written-off debt, stipulations are put into their buy-sell agreement. These agreements may contain one of these two provisions: the agreement will either state that if the debt collector sues the consumer, the creditor cannot be contacted to assist with litigation, or alternatively, the debt collector must pay all the costs and per diem fees to send out one of the creditor's employees to testify about the debt. These agreements are kept under lock and key, but in reality, this is the kind of thing that they say.

In other words, creditors will not help debt buyers *verify* the debt even though they are the only ones qualified as a matter of law to verify it. Not only are debt buyers unable to obtain assistance from the creditor once they buy it but also, they may have never received any original account-level documentation from the creditor of the debt in the first place! I've seen cases where the only thing that a debt buyer receives is a spreadsheet containing names, phone numbers and amounts owed. This alone cannot verify a debt.

* * *

Let's return now to the main point: trade lines that appear on a credit report must be accurate *and* verifiable. If they cannot be verified, they must be deleted. Is there somewhere in the FCRA where it says this? Yes! It can be found in 15 U.S.C. § 1681g. It states that a CRA must tell consumers that it is not required to remove accurate, derogatory information *unless* the information is (1) outdated *or* (2) CANNOT BE VERIFIED. This wording of the statute is a little awkward, so let's state it another way; <u>if derogatory information cannot be verified, then it must be deleted from the credit report</u>.

Let me explain this subsection of 1681g a little more. Section 1681g mandates that CRAs inform consumers of some of their rights under the law. As a general rule, derogatory information can remain on your report—you cannot force a CRA to remove accurate, derogatory. HOWEVER, there are two exceptions to this general rule. First, a consumer has the right to remove accurate-but-outdated information. The definition of outdated-but-accurate information is found in section 1681c. Second, the other exception is accurate information that CANNOT BE VERIFIED.

Now that that has been explained twice, let's summarize this important point, but more forcefully:

CONSUMERS HAVE THE RIGHT TO FORCE CRAs TO REMOVE INFORMATION FROM THEIR CREDIT REPORTS THAT, ALTHOUGH ACCURATE, CANNOT BE VERIFIED.

IF A CRA OR FURNISHER DID NOT VERIFY INFORMATION (LIKE AN UNPAID DEBT) BEFORE LISTING IT AND YOU ASK THEM TO VERIFY IT, AND THEY CANNOT, WILL NOT OR DO NOT DO IT, THEY MUST DELETE THE INFORMATION. IT IS A VIOLATION OF THE FCRA FOR A CRA OR FURNISHER TO CONTINUE TO REPORT INFORMATION THAT THEY HAVE NOT, CANNOT, OR WILL NOT VERIFY. IT IS A WILLFUL VIOLATION IF THEY KNOWINGLY DO NOT VERIFY and CONTINUE TO REPORT IT—AFTER YOU DISPUTE IT.

* * *

It's important that you appreciate the power of this provision in the FCRA. People have written books *only* on this one provision. Because even if information on your report is accurate, it can still be removed if it cannot be verified.

Items on your credit report must be accurate and verifiable, or it must be deleted, as a matter of law.

The Right to Explain the Verification Process

Now, here's another important point, almost as important as the previous point just made:

IF A CRA REPORTS BACK THAT THE INFORMATION YOU REQUESTED TO BE VERIFIED HAS BEEN VERIFIED, YOU HAVE THE RIGHT TO ASK HOW IT WAS VERIFIED, AND THEY ARE REQUIRED TO RESPOND.

In other words, if you ask a CRA to look into the accuracy of an unpaid phone bill on your credit report, and to verify the alleged unpaid debt, if that CRA reports back that it was verified, you have the right to ask how it was verified *if it was not already provided in their response.* The statute that permits you to ask about the verification process is 15 U.S.C. 1681i(a)(6)(B)(iii).

Let's describe a simple scenario:

You find an alleged debt on your credit report that does not belong to you. Pursuant to 15 U.S.C. § 1681i(a)(1)(A), you have the right to initiate a "reinvestigation" of that item. It's called a reinvestigation, even though it's your first time disputing the item, because, presumably, an investigation was conducted by them before it was ever allowed on your report. Once the investigation is complete, 15 U.S.C. 1681i(a)(6)(B)(iii) allows you to request what was done to perform the investigation:

"...a description of the procedure used to determine the accuracy and completeness of the information shall be provided to the consumer by the agency, including the business name and address of any furnisher of information contacted in connection with such information and the telephone number of such furnisher, if reasonably available."

Failure to provide the requisite information constitutes a violation of your rights under the FCRA.

* * *

Summary

The duty of the CRA and the furnisher to verify or delete even accurate information on your credit report is a powerful duty that cannot be ignored if you exercise those rights properly.

The case law of the bench even states that if you request verification and they delete the information without a reasonable investigation, it is still a violation. The rationale is that if they investigate these claims, they can learn from what they are doing wrong and lessen the burden of future mistakes on consumers.

Once CRAs inform you that an investigation is complete, I would suggest that you do not take their word for it. Follow up with the CRA by asking them to detail the name, address, and phone number (if reasonably available) of the furnisher they contacted, as well as the procedures that were used to verify the debt.

The right of the consumer to delete accurate-yet-unverified or un-investigated disputes are among the most powerful tools in your FCRA arsenal to clean up your credit report.

CHAPTER 6: TAKING THE FIRST STEP: REQUESTING FULL FILE DISCLOSURES

The first step in discovering information CRAs store about you, correcting errors in your consumer files, (including credit reports), and seeing who is pulling information from your consumer files, is to request a disclosure of "all information" in your consumer files.

Chances are that the CRAs will respond by sending you a credit report, but this is an error on their part. As we have discussed earlier in this book, your consumer file contains more information than what is found on the credit report. In your *entire consumer file* will be information about your criminal history, and other types of personal information that will not show up on a consumer's credit report, yet the information is still sold to other users who are making decisions about you regarding insurance, extending credit, employment, licensing, and government security clearances.

* * *

In this book's Foreword, I stated that the *Consumer Reporting Agencies (CRAs) are collecting and selling all of the information about you that they can to everyone they can (legally, and sometimes illegally).* When we talk about CRAs, we tend to focus on the three nationwide CRAs (Equifax, Experian, and TransUnion), but there are over 50 other CRAs operating in America, selling specialized information about consumers to buyers. Specialized CRAs focus on such areas as insurance, property, tenant screening, employment and background checks, medical care, utilities usage, and banking matters. You can obtain a free copy of these other CRAs by going to CreditFixPower.com and signing up for the free membership.

If all you receive is a credit report, is that a "full file disclosure?" No! If you want proof, do this: (1) order your Full File Disclosure from LexisNexis (see instructions below); (2) order your credit reports. You will see that your full file disclosure from LexisNexis may be over 100 pages, while your credit report will be around 15 or 20. Some of my clients have noted that some of the items that appear on their LexisNexis report come from the CRAs, but when they look on their reports from the CRAs, that information is missing. This is proof positive that the CRAs have more information about you than what is on your credit report.

In the earlier chapter entitled, "Consumer Files and Reports v. Credit Files and Reports," the distinction was made between your *Consumer Files v. Credit Files*, and *Consumer Reports v. Credit Reports*.

Each CRA maintains a *consumer file* on consumers. From that information, they generate various *reports*, including various types of *consumer reports.*

Federal law states that you're entitled to receive "all information" in your consumer file. 15 U.S.C. § 1681g(a) states the following relevant information:

"Every consumer reporting agency shall, upon request, and subject to section 1681h(a)(1) of this title, clearly and accurately disclose to the consumer...***all information in the consumer's file*** at the time of the request[.]"

Except for LexisNexis, CRAs generally will *not* give you your entire *consumer* file even if you ask for it. After you ask for everything in your consumer file, the CRAs will send you back an answer like this (sarcastic embellishment added). "We received your request for your *full disclosure of your consumer file.* But WE KNOW what you MEANT to say: you actually just wanted your credit report. So, here's your free annual copy of your credit report. YOU'RE WELCOME!"

When CRAs are sued over this issue, I have witnessed them tell the courts that the only thing they are required to turn over is your credit report, even though you requested clearly the entire contents of your consumer file. CRAs try and conflate the two concepts.

Don't settle for a credit report after you've asked for full file disclosure. Write back and tell them that they did not send you what you asked for.

* * *

Types of Information that CRAs Could Have in Their Consumer Files

Remember that, in the *Millstone* case, the information in Mr.

Millstone's consumer file that was included into a consumer report that caused the cancellation of his insurance was that he was labeled as a "hippy type" and "suspected drug user"! The information that led to his cancellation had nothing to do with his credit cards, account balances, or credit history.

To obtain Full File Disclosure from LexisNexis, follow these steps:

A. https://personalreports.lexisnexis.com/access_your_full_file_disclosure.jsp

B. Read the instructions: https://personalreports.lexisnexis.com/pdfs/CD107_CP-File-Disclosure-Request-Form_pg-1.pdf

C. Download their FULL-FILE

D. Disclosure Request form here:

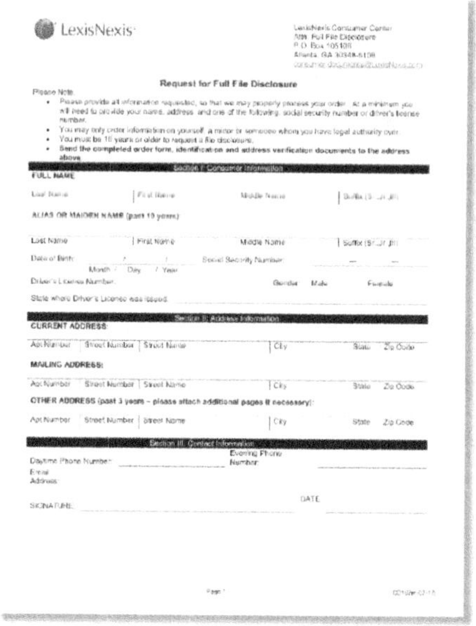

LexisNexis

LexisNexis Consumer Center
Attn: Full File Disclosure
P.O. Box 105108
Atlanta, GA 30348-5108

Request for Full File Disclosure

Please Note:

- Please provide all information requested, so that we may properly process your order. At a minimum you will need to provide your name, address and one of the following: social security number or driver's license number.
- You may only order information on yourself, a minor or someone whom you have legal authority over.
- You must be 18 years or older to request a file disclosure.
- **Send the completed order form, identification and address verification documents to the address above.**

Section I: Consumer Information

FULL NAME

Last Name | First Name | Middle Name | Suffix (Sr., Jr., III)

ALIAS OR MAIDEN NAME (past 10 years)

Last Name | First Name | Middle Name | Suffix (Sr., Jr., III)

Date of Birth: Month / Day / Year   Social Security Number:

Driver's License Number: Gender: Male Female

State where Driver's License was issued:

Section II: Address Information

CURRENT ADDRESS:

Apt Number | Street Number | Street Name | City | State | Zip Code

MAILING ADDRESS:

Apt Number | Street Number | Street Name | City | State | Zip Code

OTHER ADDRESS (past 3 years – please attach additional pages if necessary):

Apt Number | Street Number | Street Name | City | State | Zip Code

Section III: Contact Information

Daytime Phone Number: Evening Phone Number:

Email Address:

SIGNATURE: DATE

Page 1

Disclosure Request Form from LexisNexis

https://personalreports.lexisnexis.com/pdfs/CD107_CP-

File-Disclosure-Request-Form_pg-3.pdf

Submit Questions to LexisNexis:

https://personalreports.custhelp.com/app/ask.

After you receive your LexisNexis Report, and responses to your requests for full file disclosures from the other CRAs, if you are sent consumer credit reports *only*, then further action is required. See the asterisked comment below.

Make a Second (and Final) Request. If the CRAs send you a consumer credit report in response to your request for full file disclosure, then you should ask *again*. Remember: they might say, when they send you a consumer credit report, words to this effect, "Here's the credit report that you requested." You need to correct them in a second letter, saying in effect, "Hey! I didn't ask for my consumer credit report! I asked for all of the information contained in my consumer files. This is unacceptable! Send me the full file disclosure you are required to send me pursuant to 15 U.S.C. § 1681g." They will be out of excuses if you make this second request and they continue to ignore you. Now, the violations may be willful and knowing which, if they are, can subject them to punitive damages in a lawsuit.

If a CRA will not give you a full file disclosure of all of the information contained in your consumer file, then you only have one other option if you want it, which is to sue them, and force them to give it up.

* * *

* After you have requested full file disclosures, ordering your credit reports online is the next step. This may seem like an unnecessary step, since (unless they change their ways soon) you

probably received credit reports in response to your requests for full file disclosure. Ask for them anyway—you don't want the CRAs to later claim that you were "confused" when you asked them for a full file disclosure. Show them you know the difference by asking for each consumer credit report separately. Ordering these reports and knowing what to do with them is covered in the next chapter.

CHAPTER 7: REQUESTING CREDIT REPORTS

After you have made your requests for full file disclosure from each CRA, and from LexisNexis, you need to order copies of your credit reports—even if they improperly sent you consumer credit reports in response to your requests for full file disclosure. To order your consumer reports, do not go to this site: freecreditreport.com. Also, do not rely on reports older than 60 days—you'll need fresh reports! Finally, do not use tri-merge reports or other specialty reports. Use only separate credit reports from each CRA.

* * *

How to Order Your Reports

The best place to go to order current, updated reports is the website that the federal government *required* the CRAs to set up to offer free reports to consumers once a year:

Annualcreditreport.com

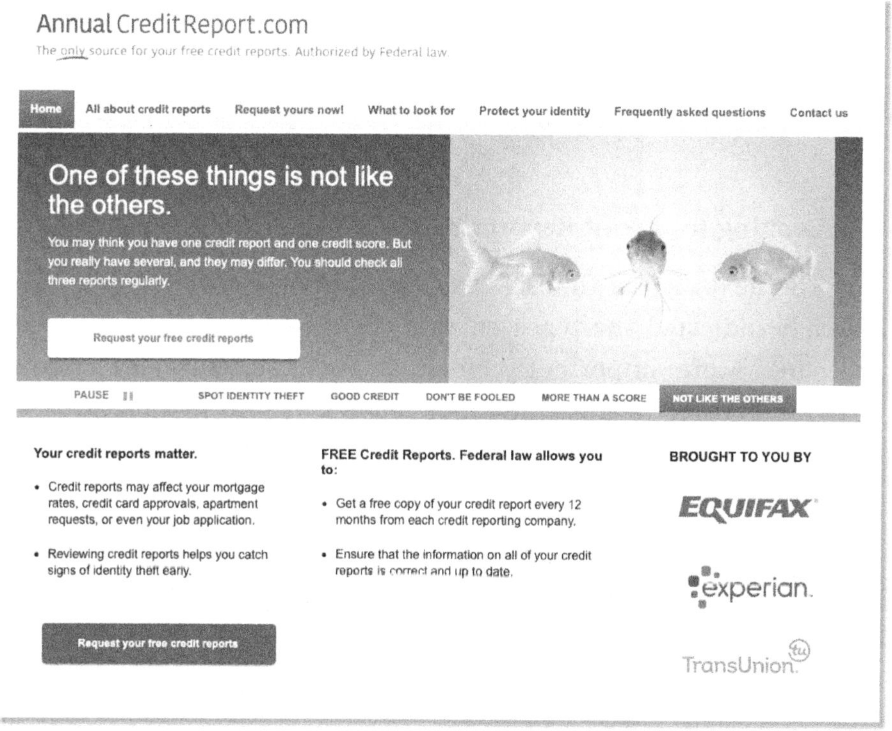

When you order your reports online, you will be able to download them immediately. Warning: they will ask you a series of questions to make sure you are who you say you are before you can download each report. Ironically, these questions come from your credit reports! So be prepared to remember how much your mortgage payment is, your auto loan, the names of banks from which the loans were secured, etc.

How Long Do CRAs and Furnishers Have to Respond?

When you send out dispute letters, CRAs normally have 30 days to respond to your dispute. However, the CFPB has stated that if you order your reports from AnnualCreditReport.com, they have an additional 15 days to respond, or 45 days total. Although I could not find any evidence in the FCRA for this extension of time, I suggest you follow the CFPB's stated position on the matter and allow 45 days for a response.

* * *

Looking for Credit Report Errors

The next step in finding errors is to review your reports. I have already indicated the types of errors normally found. Look at each account. More importantly, look at each account and compare what's reported against the other reports. If information about the same account differs from report to report, then you know there is an error somewhere.

At the end of the report are "Inquiries." These are companies, and possibly individuals, who accessed your reports. Make sure that you know who they are.

Reading reports can be a little tricky at first. Each credit report agency uses their own abbreviations and so they are not consistent between each other. You need to learn the abbreviations and vernacular used by each consumer reporting agency. These can be looked up online. You're looking at the dates on which the account was opened and closed, correct balance information, correct payment history, any late pays, past dues, or any other inaccurate account information. You also need to make sure that your name is correct, your residence or residences, and other personal information. One of the common failures to update is if you had a bankruptcy and the furnishers did not update the status showing a balance owed, when in fact the balance was discharged in bankruptcy.

It's important that you understand the steps of this and the previous chapter, on how to make your requests, in what order, and what to do after you receive them.

1. Order a request for full file disclosure from LexisNexis;
2. Order a request for full file disclosure from each consumer reporting agency. Expect that they will not comply, and that they will only send you consumer credit reports;
3. Make a second request for full file disclosure; tell each one who only gave you a consumer credit file that they did not give you what was required, pursuant to 15 U.S.C. 1681g;
4. Go online to annualcreditreport.com and order copies of your credit reports online; and
5. Review each for errors and potential impermissible users;
6. Compare—find any differences between these reports and the full credit file disclosure provided by LexisNexis; and
7. Look for errors and violations—which is the subject of the next chapter.

CHAPTER 8: COMMON ERRORS AND VIOLATIONS

In this chapter, we deal with common errors that may appear on your credit report(s). Remember, these credit reports are generated by CRAs. When most people think of consumer reporting agencies, they think of the three national consumer reporting agencies, namely, Equifax, Experian, and TransUnion. However, there are over 50 consumer reporting agencies operating within the United States. (To get a list of their names, addresses and websites for free, go to Chapter 15.) When you hear the term "background check" for employment, the term is referring to a consumer reporting agency that specializes in criminal background information about job applicants, for example. This "background check" company is still a CRA because it fits the definition provided by the FCRA.

The following list is organized by commonality of errors, beginning with the most prevalent. This information was acquired from the Consumer Financial Protection Bureau (CFPB). To visit their website, visit https://www.consumerfinance.gov.

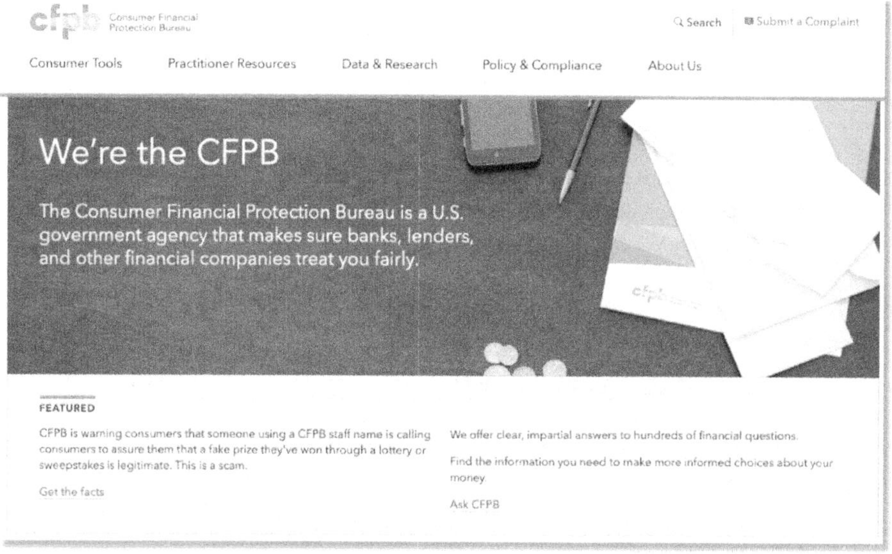

Common Reporting Errors

The CRAs use 30 dispute codes to categorize the nature of your dispute. A comprehensive list (as of 2016) is provided in Appendix 4. A brief description of the most common types of errors is also provided below:

1. **Not His or Hers. Mixed Information**. Information belonging to someone else is placed in the wrong person's consumer file. Believe it or not, this is the most common type of error on a credit report.

2. **Dispute of Account/Status History.** After a consumer has disputed information on her or his credit report, notification of the dispute should appear on the reports. Failure to note the dispute on the report after it is reported is the second most common mistake on a credit report.

3. **Inaccurate Information**. Misinformation is the third most common error on a credit report. Such information includes but is not limited to where a consumer lived, the spelling of her/his name, alleged addresses, account numbers, etc. These may be the result of clerical errors during data input or transmission.

4. **Disputed Amounts.** Sometimes, credit reports show wrong balances owed to creditors. This is readily observed when comparing one report with another. For example, comparing one's Equifax report with a TransUnion report, each reporting a different amount owed, shows that one or both of them are reflecting inaccurate information.

5. **Claims of Closed Accounts.** Some mistakes relate to a closed account, with the accompanying statement that it was closed by the consumer, when it was not.

INCORRECT INFORMATION BY CATEGORY	**PERCENT**
Not His or Hers	31%
Disputes Account Status/History	21%
Inaccurate Info. Non-Specific Dispute	17%
Disputed Amounts Reported	9%

Claims Account Closed By Consumer	7%
Other	15%
Total	100%

The remaining types of errors represent approximately 15 percent of the remaining reporting problems:

6. **Old, Negative Information is Not Removed**. Debts older than 7 years should not be on a consumer's credit report. Bankruptcies should also drop off after 10 years.
7. **Failure to update the current status of a debt.** Sometimes, furnishers or consumer reporting agencies fail to update information that they are reporting, such as paid in full on an account that was previously not paid. Other common remarks about status include whether an account has gone to collections or has been charged off.

Now that we have discussed the various errors, and the most common types, you should be able to spot them as you review your credit reports. The next chapter will briefly cover how to order your credit reports, and how NOT to order them.

Common Violations

You might recall that in Chapter 4, I pointed out that there are two broad categories of FCRA violations: violations that have already occurred as a matter of law (whether or not you do anything), and violations that occur when you exercise your rights under the FCRA and the CRAs and/or furnishers fail to respond or do not respond in full compliance with the law (i.e., after you *do* something).

In the next two chapters, we'll cover the latter scenario—what you need to *do correctly* to exercise your rights under the FCRA. In this section on common violations, we take a deeper look at violations you might spot after receiving both your full file disclosure (at least the one from LexisNexis) and your consumer credit reports.

A. **Proof of Failure to Provide Full File Disclosures**. If you find items in your lengthy LexisNexis report that come from a CRA but are not also found on your consumer credit report, then you have just proven that there is a consumer file with information on it that is not showing up on your consumer credit report. In other words, you have proven that a CRA has violated the full file disclosure requirements of 15 U.S.C. § 1681g. Here's an example. Let's say your LexisNexis report shows that you have an open credit account with Discover Card with a paid-off balance of zero. LexisNexis states that the source of this information came from Experian. However, on your Experian consumer credit report, the Discover account does not show up at all. This would prove that Experian has data in its consumer files that is not showing up on your consumer credit report; when it failed to disclose all of the information in its consumer files about you, it broke the law.

B. **Failing to Follow Proper Procedures**. Even though a CRA is not in violation of the law for reporting false or erroneous information unless you dispute the information, each CRA still owes a duty to follow reasonable procedures to ensure maximum accuracy of your credit report. Sometimes you can tell whether they are following reasonable procedures by the type of information that is appearing on your report. As you review your report, ask yourself this question: "Could this information have been placed on my report if the CRA was following reasonable procedures?" If the answer is no, then the CRA may have violated 15 U.S.C. § 1681b.

Here's an example of a Section 1681b violation. Bankruptcies are supposed to drop off after 10 years. The CRAs know this. If it stays on longer than 10 years then they are not using reasonable procedures to ensure maximum accuracy.

C. **Improper Inquiries**. There is a section on your credit reports, usually towards the end of your report, that shows who recently pulled your credit report. Sometimes you will see names on there of persons or entities who had no reason, no permissible purpose, for accessing your consumer files. If they did not have a legal reason, they are in violation of 15 U.S.C. 1681b. This is covered in more depth in Chapter 11.

Once you've found errors and/or violations, you are ready to begin writing letters to furnishers of information, CRAs, and users to rectify errors and pursue them for violations. The next chapter will give you a broad overview on how to conduct yourself in a manner that is in compliance with the FCRA.

CHAPTER 9: CONDUCTING A FCRA-COMPLIANT CAMPAIGN

The FCRA has no power to help or protect you, unless you *comply* with the *requirements* of the law. Once you follow those requirements, you are empowered, because you can force the FCRA to (1) turn things over they refused to give you, (2) correct ignored errors and (3) seek monetary damages.

Using the Law to Enforce Your Rights

Filing a lawsuit against violators is your last resort, but at least it is an option that is available to you if you have taken all of the necessary steps and remain ignored. Sometimes, in some cases, you won't have any other choice. But before we get into enforcement through litigation, you should have completed the following:

1. You've made a request for full file disclosure from LexisNexis, and received it;

2. You've made a request for full file disclosure from all three national CRAs (and others), and received something back;

3. You've made a *second* request for full file disclosure from every CRA to whom you've made the first request, but did not receive a proper response;

4. You've made a separate request for each of your credit reports from Equifax, Experian, and TransUnion, and any other CRA you may want to query, and received them or were ignored;

5. You've thoroughly reviewed each report, comparing them against one another for errors or impermissible uses, for such things as the following:

- Information that is not yours;
- Information that is incorrect;
- Information that is too old;
- Inquiries from businesses or persons with whom you are not familiar;
- Anything else that looks erroneous, unclear, or looks like it should be deleted or corrected; and/or
- Violations of the FCRA that have already been committed.

6. You have found errors that require correction or deletion, and/or you did not receive full file disclosures from each of the CRAs.

* * *

Beginning the Enforcement Process

After taking these preliminary steps, you are now ready to start contacting the CRAs and furnishers. Remember these three groups that you can challenge: furnishers, CRAs, and users. Furnishers report information to CRAs, CRAs gather and disseminate information about you, and users buy this information from the CRAs. The law permits you to approach these entities two different ways—using a direct approach or an indirect approach.

When a CRA reports erroneous information, you are required to write them and request a correction or deletion. The FCRA does not require them to fix an error until you write to them. Furnishers of information are often the source of the errors, but not always. In order to correct errors by furnishers, you can use one of two approaches, depending upon the type of correction you are seeking—the direct approach or the indirect approach. The direct approach is writing directly to the furnisher of the erroneous information. The indirect approach is writing to the FCRAs and asking them to notify the furnishers of a need for correction.

Under the FCRA, you are not allowed to contact a furnisher directly; you must go through the CRAs. However, the Code of Federal Regulations (CFR), which are rules enacted by federal administrative agencies, allow for limited kinds of direct disputes by consumers to furnishers, such as creditors and debt collectors--for limited types of disputes. Let's discuss each one.

* * *

The Direct Approach with Furnishers

16 C.F.R. § 660.4 permits consumers to make direct disputes to furnishers (creditors) in four scenarios. For example, Section 660.4(a)(4) says consumers can make direct disputes to furnishers when it involves a "consumer's performance or other conduct concerning an account." Other grounds for making a direct dispute

to a furnisher include identity theft and fraud, payment and balance history, or current balance of an account with a creditor. You can also take a direct approach with users when they obtain your reports without a permissible purpose.

* * *

The Direct Approach with Users (People who pull your credit report): Limited Use

When you look at the "Inquiries" section of your credit report and see someone pulling your credit report without a valid reason, you can write directly to that user and ask them why they were permitted to access your credit report.

* * *

The Indirect Approach: The General Approach

If you are using the FCRA to request deletions or corrections from furnishers, you must write letters directly to the CRAs only, even if you need to correct an error made by the furnisher who is supplying the information. <u>There is no provision in the FCRA that allows you to directly require a furnisher to conduct a reasonable investigation into your request for corrections or deletions</u>; it can only be done indirectly.

Steps to Using the Indirect Approach Via the FCRA

Below is a summary of the next steps that you need to follow using the FCRA:

1. Send letters of dispute (or copies of letters you are sending) to the furnishers, who are usually original creditors, debt collectors or debt buyers; and then

2. Send letters of dispute to the CRAs who are reporting erroneous information *three days after* the dispute letters to the furnisher were sent. The CRAs are required to respond to your request within 30 to 45 days.

* * *

The way the FCRA works, furnishers are not required to respond directly to the disputes of consumers. Instead, furnishers must only respond to disputes made when they come from the CRA to them. That is the way the FCRA has set it up. However, sometimes furnishers claim they did not get a sufficient explanation of the dispute from the CRA, so if you send them a detailed letter of the problem you effectively end this problem/excuse. (Creditors are usually businesses who let you buy things without paying cash: credit card companies, banks, automobile lenders, home mortgages, utility companies, landlords and insurance companies—to name a few of the more obvious ones. Debt collectors are those who acquire a debt or are collecting a debt on behalf of unpaid creditors.)

Remember, under the FCRA, furnishers don't have to respond to a dispute letter sent directly to them by you; however, once again, the letter is important because (a) it puts them on notice of the error and (b) prevents them from making an excuse later that they did not understand the reasons for the needing to conduct a re-investigation after a CRA contacts them. Write the letter 3-5 days before notifying any of the CRAs in writing.

In the next chapter, we'll cover the dos and don'ts of letter writing.

CHAPTER 10: PREPARING DISPUTE LETTERS

Writing letters to the CRAs is the most important step of the dispute process. In this chapter, I'll make recommendations of things to do and things that you should not do.

* * *

Writing Dispute Letters to Furnishers

Previously, I recommended that you send a letter to the furnisher first, even though they do not have the duty to *act* on your letter. The letter is sent for another purpose: to provide *notice* of the problem so they can't later say that they were not fully informed about the nature of the dispute.

You can send the furnisher an exact copy of what you're going to send to the CRAs if the letter deals only with the furnisher's mistake. But if your CRA letter talks about multiple violations with other furnishers in the same letter, it's better that you write the furnisher a separate letter, than to send them a copy of the one you sent the CRA.

If you send the furnisher a copy of the letter you wrote to the CRA, then you should include a cover letter explaining what it is and why you're providing it. "Enclosed please find a copy of the letter I am sending to Equifax to dispute the information you provided to them."

* * *

Technical Considerations in Writing Letters to CRAs

If you want to use methods that work, then every dispute letter written must contain the following information in order to exercise your rights under the FCRA, if the CRAs violate the law.

1. Write or print your letters on paper to create an evidence trail. CRAs offer online tools to submit your disputes. Do *not* use these online dispute methods offered by the CRAs, for two reasons. First, you won't have a paper trail of what you did, no record of submitting your dispute. How are you going to prove they overlooked or willfully ignored their statutory duty in the absence of proof? Second, some CRAs allow you to use their online services *only if* you agree to waive your rights under the FCRA to file a private right of action, and agree to solve their violation of the law through binding arbitration pursuant to the Federal Arbitration Act, https://www.law.cornell.edu/uscode/text/9. You don't want to waive your right to sue under the FCRA. If you have already disputed these items online, switch over immediately to writing disputes in printed or handwritten letter form from this point forward.

2. Date the letter. This may seem like an obvious thing, but you want to keep a record of when the letter was written and sent.

3. Mail the letters to the correct addresses. Here are the correct addresses for sending letters to the three national CRAs:

Experian Information Solutions, Inc.
P.O. Box 2002
Allen, TX 75013-2000

Equifax Information Services LLC
P.O. Box 740256
Atlanta, GA 30374

TransUnion, LLC
P.O. Box 2000
Chester, PA 19016

4. Send the Letters via Certified Mail. Do NOT send only First-Class mail; otherwise, you will lose your paper trail. Send your letter *only* by way of certified mail through the U.S. Postal Service. There are two ways that you can send out these letters. First is Certified Mail, *Return Receipt Requested.* This involves attaching a green card to the back of the letter; then the Postal Service Worker hands the letter to the CRA and you are sent back through the mail a stamped or signed for green card as proof of delivery. Alternatively, you can simply send the letter "Certified Mail" *without* "return receipt requested." Each certified letter has a tracking number. You can go online to USPS.gov and track the delivery of the letter online. It's also cheaper not to use the *return receipt requested* option.

5. Keep Physical Copies of the Letter and Proof of Delivery. Keep a copy of every letter you send. Put the Certified Letter on the letter before you send it. Keep the green card safe if you requested return receipt and make a copy of it on 8.5 x 11-inch paper to give to an attorney later. Alternatively, PRINT OUT a copy of screenshots from the USPS website showing that the delivery was successful. Finally, keep the receipt with the ***tracking number*** when you first prepared the letter, and make a photocopy of it, too. *The letter with a tracking number, the receipt and either the return receipt or the USPS.gov website tracking printouts should all have the same certified mail receipt number.*

6. How to Send Via Certified Mail. If you do not know how to send a certified letter, various instructions can be found on YouTube.com, where there are several videos people have made that will show you how to properly do it. Do a search for "USPS Tracking."

7. Put Your Name and Address on the Letter. You need to put your name and return address on the letter so that the CRA will know where to respond to the request. I recommend putting them on the top, centered, or down by your signature at the bottom of the letter.

8. Provide Proof of Who You Are and Where You Live. The CRAs want to make sure you are who you say you are, so they want two things to confirm this. There are two ways to do this. Sample letters provided by the FTC and CFPB merely use the Report confirmation number, date of birth, address, phone number, and "anything else they request." This may suffice but it leaves it opened ended for other requests for information, and therefore, more delays. A second way of doing this is to provide a copy of a valid, government-issued ID with your photo on it. This is usually your driver's license or state identification card if you do not drive, issued by the Department of Motor Vehicles in your state. In addition, CRAs want proof of residency. Your name on any utility bill at the address where you live is perfect. If your name is not on a utility bill, you will need to come up with something else. One other way is to send an affidavit signed by a notary public before whom you appear in your county and state. You could use property records with your name on it, or maybe even your registration for your car. DO NOT give them your social security card OR your birth certificate. These are not necessary to comply with CRA protocols for proof of identity and residency. For furnishers (creditors or debt collectors) that you contact directly, include your account number. *HOT TIP: If you've already ordered your report, it comes with a reference number. You may be able to use that instead of proof of identity and residency, since you have already been through the screening process. This method is used in certain form letters create by the CFPB.*

9. You or Your Attorney Should Prepare and Send the Dispute Letter(s)—no one else. The FCRA states that the *consumer* must dispute the errors. Some attorneys who defend the CRAs in litigation argue that a dispute letter sent by someone else on behalf of the consumer, such as a Credit Repair Organization (or "CRO") does not trigger a violation because it was not sent *by* the consumer. Although I do not agree with the interpretation of these defense attorneys, you can avoid the issue by preparing and mailing them yourself or hire an attorney to do it for you--someone who has legal *power of attorney* to act on your behalf. This is one of the services that my firm offers that is discussed in detail in the last chapter of this book.

* * *

The Contents of Your Letter to the CRAs

Now that we've covered the technical aspects of writing your letters to the CRAs, let's examine what your letters should say, after you have dated the letter, added the certified mail receipt number, and used the proper address of the CRA.

Be clear and concise. Identify the problem you found on that CRA's report. "Your report states that my name is Carl." "Your report states that I still owe Capital One $1,000." "According to your report, I have a credit card with Bank of America."

1. Explain why that item is incorrect. "My name is Carlos, not Carl." "I do not have an outstanding balance with Capital One; I paid it off last January." "I do not have a credit card with Bank of America."
2. Tell them what you want them to do. "Please correct the spelling of my name." "Please investigate and change the balance of the card to $0." "Please delete this reference to a Bank of America credit card."
3. Add any additional items in your letter that you found.
4. Attach documents in support of your claim, if you have them. "Here is a copy of my bill and the canceled check showing I paid Dr. Gruber's bill in full." You should also send back a copy of your credit report with the items circled that are in dispute. CRAs can now attach those documents when they notify furnishers that an item is in dispute, so be sure to take advantage of this. Warning: even though "e-Oscar," which is the system CRAs use to communicate with furnishers, now allows for attachments, it does not mean they will actually utilize this feature. For a complete list of all credit dispute codes used between CRAs and Furnishers, go to Appendix 6.
5. Tell them you expect an answer in 45 days if you ordered your credit reports from AnnualCreditReport.com (30 days if your ordered them by phone or in writing). "Please respond to this letter within 45 days of receipt of this letter."

6. Attach proof of identity, proof of residency, and any other documents that will establish your claim.

* * *

Do Not Do Any of the Following:

- DO NOT use online dispute reporting methods offered by a CRA.
- DO NOT send your birth certificate.
- DO NOT use the phone to orally call in disputes.
- DO NOT send letters First Class Mail without being certified.
- DO NOT send letters without proof of identity and residency.
- DO NOT forget to keep copies of everything you send.

Many of the books that deal with letter writing contain samples that you must type up from the pages of the book. We've made the process even easier; simply go to CreditFixPower.com and sign up as a free member. You will then have access to download sample letters in Microsoft Word form (.docx) that will make it much easier for you to prepare your letters. We call these Power Tools, and they're included in our Tier One service, which is the purchase of this book. For access to all the letters and instructions for every type of situation explained in this book, you can upgrade to the second option, which includes the entire Credit Fix Power Toolbox.

CHAPTER 11: PERMISSIBLE AND IMPERMISSIBLE PULLS

When can a consumer report be "pulled" or accessed by a user? The answer is found in 15 U.S.C. § 1681b; Consumer Reporting Agencies (CRAs) are supposed to screen potential users and buyers of information about consumers that is contained in consumer files. Additionally, the persons or entities who want to access that information must have a permissible purpose.

* * *

Permissible Purposes or "Pulls"

Proper users who are permitted to look at information pulled from your consumer file generally include the following: (a) a potential creditor who wants to extend credit to you, (b) existing creditors who want to make sure you can still afford to make your payments on existing debts, (c) employers (who obtain written permission first), (d) insurance underwriters, (e) government entities seeking to grant you a license, (f) a business transaction initiated by a consumer, and (g) child support obligations. For exact details, study 15 U.S.C. § 1681b. Those purposes are set forth in this section. It states that there are NO OTHER PERMISSIBLE PURPOSES for which these reports can be requested, unless it is listed in this section.

After obtaining consumer credit files and reports, inquiries will show up on these reports. Some of them will be familiar to the consumer. Some will not.

A consumer may challenge or question any unauthorized or unfamiliar inquiries from the person(s) or entity(ies) making the inquiry(ies).

If someone pulls a consumer's report without a permissible purpose, one or two parties may be liable for damages to the consumer:

1. Consumer Reporting Agencies who have not properly investigated the background of the Inquirer or the reason for wanting the report; and/or
2. The Inquirer who claimed to have a legitimate purpose pursuant to Section 1681b but did not.

Let's go over how you spot possible impermissible uses and what to do if you think you spot one:

Go to the "Inquiries" section of your credit report. Look for any unusual user names who pulled your report.

Write a letter to the user and ask them why they pulled your report. Make your letter a time-dated letter, i.e., give them a reasonable deadline in which to answer. Look at the next chapter on preserving evidence to know how to properly document your request.

It's important to understand "hard pulls" and "soft pulls." The FCRA uses no such terminology, but it still helps to distinguish those that allegedly have no effect on your credit score (soft pulls) from pulls that affect your credit score (hard pulls).

Hard Pulls (Inquiries). With hard pulls, the following information is being given to users:

- Full Credit Reports;
- Credit Scores – although different scoring models are used (there are many kinds of FICO scores, for example); and
- Criminal background information in employment inquiries; driving records too.

Reports contain a staggering amount of information about us!

Soft Pulls (Inquiries). Soft Pulls share the following information with users:

- Limited information about you, such as demographics;
- Basic "qualifying" information; and
- Promotional inquiries made to you where you just made it on a promo list.

Generally, only hard-pull cases should be pursued in court.

Legal Pulls. Section 1681b sets forth pulls that are legally permissible. Make sure you do not write to the CRAs and question pulls that are permitted by the statute. Here are some examples of permissible pulls:

1. A potential creditor pulls a credit report after a consumer applies for credit with that creditor;
2. A consumer applies for insurance, and the insurance company pulls her or his credit report;
3. A consumer applies for employment, and the employer pulls his or her credit report; or
4. A business pulls a consumer's credit report for some other "legitimate business need."

* * *

Legitimate Business Needs? The last permissible purpose on the list above is a *legitimate business need.* The term is a catch all, and it is broadly written. What are legitimate business needs? Here are some examples of legitimate business needs:

1. **Payment by check**. A consumer wishing to pay by check while checking out an item for purchase at a department store. *Estiverne v. Sak's Fifth Avenue*, 9 F.3d 1171 (5th Cir. 1993);
2. **Debt Collectors**. Debt collectors seeking to collect debts. *Smith v. Encore Capital Group Inc.*, 996 F. Supp. 2d (E.D. Wis. 2013). However, some argue that a debt collector who is collecting on behalf of a creditor is a legitimate pull, but a debt collector who has purchased the debt and owns it does not have a legitimate business need;
3. **Account Reviews.** Reviews on current, open credit cards. 15 U.S.C. § 1681b(a)(3)(F)(ii); and
4. **Buying a Car**. A consumer buying a vehicle at a dealership and paying by either personal check or credit card.

* * *

Business Needs That Are Not Legitimate. Here are three examples of things that are not legitimate business needs:

1. An employer who looks at a former employee's credit report to investigate embezzlement. *Russell v. Shelter Financial Services*, 604 F. Supp. 201 (W.D. Mo. 1994).
2. A lender who reviews a consumer report after the consumer had discharged the lender's loan in bankruptcy. *Godby v. Wells Fargo Bank, N.A.*, 599 F. Supp.2d 934 (S.D. Ohio 2008).
3. Spouses who pull each other's credit reports in divorce proceedings. *Cole v. American Family Mut. Ins. Co.*, 410 F. Supp. 2d 1020 (D. Kan. 2006).

Flowchart. Here is a flowchart of how to analyze permissible pulls:

- Your credit is pulled.
- Was the pull permissible?
- If yes, then END the inquiry.
- If no, then ask:
- Was it a negligent pull? If yes, then were there damages? If yes, then a lawsuit is viable. If there are no damages, a lawsuit may not be viable.
- Was it a willful impermissible pull? If yes, then a lawsuit may be viable.

* * *

Summary

All types of companies can permissibly pull a consumer's credit reports: potential and current creditors, insurers, and employers. Certain stores and vendors, and virtually anyone with whom we engage in a business transaction wherein there would be a legitimate need can also permissibly pull credit reports.

Consumer reports can contain all types of information, from simple demographics and basic qualifying information to complete credit and criminal records.

Review the inquiry sections of your credit report. Focus on the "hard" inquiries, not the soft ones. Make sure you can establish at least negligence, but make sure you can articulate damages.

CHAPTER 12: PRESERVING EVIDENCE OF FCRA VIOLATIONS

If a CRA does not honor your request for correction, deletion or verification, you or your attorney will eventually need to consider going to court if (a) your rights are violated and (b) the violator(s) will not compensate you for your statutory and financial damages. In a lawsuit, you are called the Plaintiff; the parties you are suing are called the Defendants.

In a lawsuit, the Plaintiff has the burden of proving her or his case. The only way to prove a case is by using admissible evidence. An entire body of law is devoted to what evidence is admissible at trial.

The purposes of this section are to familiarize you with what evidence you need to preserve in your case, how to properly preserve it, and how to use it to support your case. You may want to consider hiring a lawyer to help you through the process.

One of the things you must do is anticipate the objections that the Defendants will raise about your evidence, or lack of evidence. By following these steps, you will be able to make a better case, whether you are trying to settle your case out of court or whether you need to go to trial.

* * *

First, I suggest you make some "pessimistic" assumptions to get into the right mindset:

Assume the Worst. In preserving the evidence, you should presume that everyone else is going to lose evidence, and it's all up to you to preserve it. Assume the following worst-case scenarios:

1. Assume that unless your evidence is in writing or photographed, it does not exist.
2. Assume that the other side will say they never received your online submissions for correction or deletion.
3. Assume that unless you keep copies of what you write, all other copies and originals will disappear.
4. Assume that anything you are told on the telephone will be denied by the Defendants.
5. Assume that anything you say on a phone call is inadmissible at trial.
6. Assume that any phone call Defendants say is recorded will be "lost" unless it favors their version of the facts.
7. Assume that if you talk to a lawyer for the defense that they will use that conversation against you in court or deny that

certain things were said that help your case.

Given these assumptions, you need to *document everything in writing.* Do not rely on digital recordings of conversations unless you obtain permission; there are strict laws that may prevent their admissibility without permission. The laws vary from state to state. Here are some things you must do to preserve evidence:

Some of this information is repetitive because it was covered in the chapter on writing dispute letters, but the same rules and documentation apply to everything that you do. Let's go over them again.

Put Everything in Writing and On Paper (Letters) Always, Never Online (Electronically). Everything you say to them must be put in writing or confirmed in writing. Do not engage in discussions on the phone with the Defendants or their attorneys. If you must speak on the telephone, follow up the conversation with a confirming letter of what was said. Keep notes during and after every conversation. Written, audio, video or photographic evidence is the ONLY and BEST evidence you should use.

Proof of Delivery. When you send a potential defendant something in writing, do it in one of the following ways:

1. Certified Mail (put the certified number on the letter), Return Receipt Requested (Return Receipt is *optional*);

2. Certified Mail and print out proof of delivery from the USPS website (put the certified number on the letter). This is the cheapest method of documentation, but still very effective;

3. Private courier, such as Federal Express or UPS, signed for upon receipt; do not approve delivery merely left at the door; or

4. Hand-delivered, if they sign an acknowledgment of receipt of letter, which is returned to you, signed.

NEVER RELY ON REGULAR, FIRST-CLASS MAIL AS PROOF IT WAS SENT; USE ONLY CERTIFIED MAIL.

If you must litigate, keep copies of emails and proof of faxes sent to counsel for the Defendant(s).

Keep copies of everything you mail, and what you receive back. Keep complete and legible copies of everything you send to furnishers, consumer reporting agencies, and their lawyers. Keep a photocopy of exactly what you sent each of them, each time, including attachments or enclosures.

Stay Organized. With so much paper being passed around, it's important that you keep all of your paperwork organized and in a safe place.

Keep your letters organized chronologically. Keep with a copy of each letter copies of any attachments or enclosures that went along with that letter. Keep proof of delivery together with each letter.

Keep the chain of letters together. Keep with each letter the response of the CRA, furnisher, etc. Keep them in chronological order. The best practice is to keep the most recent correspondence on top, and the oldest on the bottom.

Keep the letters and replies in separate folders for each CRA, if you have multiple letters going out.

By keeping yourself organized by agency, in the event you need to consult with an attorney, you save the attorney time evaluating your case, which means you will have your lawsuit filed sooner. It will make your lawsuit go smoother.

Provide Proof of Identification and Residence with Each Letter. It's critical that you provide the Defendants with proof of who you are when you write to them. As mentioned in a previous chapter, CFPB and FTC sample letters suggest that all you need to provide is the (1) credit report confirmation number, (2) date of birth, (3) address, and (4) telephone number. They also say to provide "any other information requested." However, we have not seen any problems if the following two items are provided:

Official photographic identification. Driver's license, passport, or other official government-issued identification.

Proof of Residence. Provide a utility bill with your name and address on it. It can be your electric bill, gas bill, internet bill, etc.

CHAPTER 13: FRAUD ALERTS AND CREDIT BLOCKS OR FREEZES

The ease and benefits of the Digital Information Age come at a price: cybercrimes and identity theft. The hacks have grown in both size and frequency in recent years, they haven't become smaller and fewer. Here are just three recent examples:

In 2017, Equifax's databases were hacked, and sensitive consumer information of 145 million consumers was stolen. In 2016, over 412 million users of Adult Friend Finders were hacked. In 2013, Yahoo had data stolen for 3 billion users—the largest data breach to date. The type of data stolen is highly sought after by cyber criminals, and includes real names, email addresses, dates of birth, telephone numbers, passwords, security questions and answers, credit card data, driver's licenses, and social security numbers.

Identity theft costs individuals and companies billions of dollars annually. In 2012, identity theft cost nearly $25 billion in total losses—twice the amount of every other kind of property loss combined. Losses have declined in recent years, but with these latest breaches, the effects will be felt for years to come. *Every consumer must remain vigilant.*

With the passage of the Fair and Accurate Transactions Act (FACTA) in 2003, the identify theft provisions of the FCRA were strengthened. FACTA was merged into 15 U.S.C. § 1681 et seq., particularly sections 1681c-1 and 1681c-2, subject to limitations of liability set forth in 1681h. Other identity theft provisions are scattered throughout the FCRA.

As a consumer, two basic identity theft rights granted you under the FCRA are credit alerts and credit freezes or blocks. This chapter describes each one and how you exercise them.

The failure of a CRA to place or keep credit alerts or freezes upon your consumer files in place, after you have properly notified them of identity theft or possible identity theft, are violations of the FCRA, and if damages arise, you may be entitled to compensation.

* * *

The Business Protection Turnover Provision: 15 U.S.C. § 1681g(e)

A business that has extended credit or given goods or services to someone who is the identity thief must, within 30 days of your request, turn over to you copies of records relating to the theft, free of charge, and without a subpoena. Once you provide them proof of your identity, if they fail to turn over these records, it's a violation of the FCRA.

* * *

The Right to Fraud Alerts: 15 U.S.C. § 1681c-1

Section 1681c-1. This section is entitled "Identity Theft Protection; Fraud Alerts and Active Duty Alerts." Let's examine some of the protections now given to you, once you provide "appropriate proof of identity":

- If you have a good faith suspicion that you have or are "about to become a victim of fraud or related crime, including identity theft," you can have a fraud alert placed in your file **for 90 days**. See 15 U.S.C. § 1681c-1(a) 1.
- You can obtain free copies of consumer reports as provided by section 15 U.S.C. § 1681j(d).
- You can request a full file disclosure as required by 15 U.S.C. § 1681g. This should be provided by the CRA from whom you make the request.
- If you submit an identity theft report to a CRA on an approved form (see 15 U.S.C. § 1681a(p), the CRA can place an **extended fraud alert for up to seven years**. For the first five years, CRAs must exclude you from any "list of consumers prepared by" a CRA that is given to third parties offering credit or insurance. See 15 U.S.C. § 1681c-1(b).

Before turning now to how to block your credit, and the duties of the FCRA to block your credit, you need to begin with an identity theft complaint and affidavit. The FTC has created an Identity Theft Victim's Complaint and Affidavit website that takes you step-by-step through the process. Go here, http://ftc-identity-theft-affidavit.com, to get started. Alternatively, you can start here, https://www.identitytheft.gov.

* * *

The Right to Freeze or Block Access to Your Consumer Files: 15 U.S.C. § 1681c-2

This section of the FCRA is entitled "Block of Information Resulting from Identity Theft." This gives consumers the right to block "any information" in your consumer file that "resulted from an alleged identity theft":

- The CRAs must block the information within four days of receipt of your identification;
- You must provide appropriate proof of identity;
- The information that may be the result of identity theft must be identified by you; and
- You must provide a statement that the information is *not* related to any transaction by the consumer. See 15 U.S.C. § 1681c-2(a)

* * *

The Duty to Promptly Notify Furnishers. Once the CRA receives your notice, it must "promptly notify" the furnisher of the information of the following:

- The information that may be the result of identity theft;
- That an identity theft report was filed;
- That a block was requested; and
- The effective dates of the block. See 15 U.S.C. § 1681c-2(b)

* * *

Exceptions to Blocking; the Right to Unblock. Exceptions apply that give the CRA the power to decline or rescind your block. For example, the CRA can unblock the information if it reasonably determines that any of the following three things have occurred:

- The information was *blocked in error* or requested in error;
- The block was the result of a *material misrepresentation* by you; or
- You obtained goods or services as a result of the blocked transaction or transactions. See 15 U.S.C. § 1681c-2(c)

How to Notify the CRAs of a Freeze. You can notify the CRAs of a desire to freeze your information as follows:

- Equifax. Take Control of Your Equifax Report. https://www.equifax.com/personal/credit-report-services/, (800) 685-1111, or mail:
  - Equifax Consumer Fraud Division, PO Box 740256, Atlanta, GA 30374
- Experian: Free Security Freezes: https://www.experian.com/blogs/ask-experian/credit-education/preventing-fraud/security-freeze/, (888) 397-3742, or mail:
  - Experian, P.O. Box 9554, Allen, TX 75013
- TransUnion: Credit Help, https://www.transunion.com/credit-help, (888) 909-8872, or mail:
  - TransUnion Fraud Victim Assistance Department, P.O. Box 2000, Chester, PA 19016

* * *

The following three paragraphs come from the CFPB: https://www.consumerfinance.gov/ask-cfpb/what-does-it-mean-to-put-a-security-freeze-on-my-credit-report-en-1341/:

- A nationwide credit reporting company must place a security freeze within 1 business day of your request if made by telephone or secure electronic means. If the request is made by mail, the security freeze must be placed no later than 3 business days after receiving the request.
- A nationwide credit reporting company must send you a written confirmation of the security freeze no later than 5 business days after the security freeze is placed. They must also tell you of how to remove the security freeze.
- The nationwide consumer reporting company's webpage must also allow you to request a security freeze, an initial fraud alert, an extended fraud alert, and an active duty fraud alert.

* * *

Common Violations of FACTA (Now Part of the FCRA)

Even though you're entitled to fraud alerts, extended fraud alerts or blocking access to your consumer files, CRAs and Furnishers can sometimes make mistakes. Here is a list of the most common types of errors that have been reported:

1. **Failure to place an alert or block**. Sometimes CRAs neglect to place an alert or block access, even after you have properly notified them;

2. **Failure to keep the alert or block in place**. CRAs have been known to remove an alert or block too early; and

3. **Failure to Truncate Credit Card Numbers on Credit Card Transactions**. Credit card receipts are a "golden ticket" for thieves and fraudsters to steal your credit card information. FACTA requires all businesses to truncate credit card numbers to the last five digits.

Once again, CRAs that do not follow the statutory guidelines set forth in these sections of the FCRA can be sued for violations of the same, subject to limitations on liability.

CHAPTER 14: MAKING VIOLATORS PAY

Most of the consumers who contact my office seeking legal advice or help, come out of sheer desperation. They have tried everything that they can think of to fix something that isn't right on their credit report that is keeping them from buying a home, getting a job, or qualifying for a credit card. They've written letters, made phone calls, and in most cases, repeated these steps over and over again—in vain. Nothing seems to work.

What more can be done?

When these frustrated consumers come to my office, I can usually put them into one of three categories: (1) those who don't know what to do or how to do things the right way, (2) those who are trying to change things that can't be changed because the information rightly belongs on their credit reports and (3) those who do everything the right way, but are still ignored.

For those who don't know how to do it the right way, the preceding chapters will educate you. For those who think there's a magic trick to removing things that rightly belong on your reports, I can't offer any solutions. But for those who have done the things outlined in this book, but still suffer from the misconduct of violators, this chapter is for you.

When all else fails, you must consider filing a lawsuit or you will hit a dead end. It's your last option, and although the prospect frightens some people, it's something that you must be willing to seriously consider if you want to step out of the cycle of confusion and frustration you've been living with. Under the right conditions, it can be the most effective way to resolve your problems.

This chapter is about taking that last step—suing violators. It discusses what is involved and how to approach it. Your rights are briefly summarized at the beginning of this chapter. Next, we'll explore possible remedies—and your right to receive monetary damages. Then, we'll consider how to hire a lawyer to champion your case and discover why it's not hard to afford one. Finally, we'll discuss how sometimes cases settle, versus going to trial.

* * *

A Summary of Consumer Credit Rights

This book has explained many of the bedrock rights and protections afforded to consumers through the Fair Credit Reporting Act. Let's briefly go over them again:

- The right to expect that every CRA follows reasonable procedures in preparing a consumer report "to assure maximum possible accuracy." See 15 U.S.C. § 1681e(b);

- The right of full disclosure, to see "all information" (upon request) that is contained in your consumer files maintained by a CRA. See 15 U.S.C. § 1681g(a);
- The right to request a deletion or correction of erroneous content that is in your consumer file or on a consumer report. See 15 U.S.C. § 1681i(a)(1);
- The right to expect that a CRA *and* furnisher will conduct a reasonable investigation in response to your dispute. See 15 U.S.C. § 1681i(a)(1) and 15 U.S.C. § 1681s-2(b), respectively. Direct disputes with furnishers, under certain circumstances, are also permissible under 12 C.F.R. Part 226;
- The right to expect a reply from your dispute letter within 30 to 45 days. See 15 U.S.C. § 1681i;
- The right to have a credit alert or freeze placed in your file due to identity theft or identity theft concerns. See 15 U.S.C. § 1681c-1 and c-2; and
- The right to expect that reports generated from your consumer file, including credit reports, will not be pulled by unqualified users or used for impermissible purposes. See 15 U.S.C. § 1681b.

Throughout the previous chapters, I've shown you how to exercise each and every one of these rights correctly. However, DON'T BE DISILLUSIONED: Just because you follow all points of the law in exercising each one of your legal rights does **not** mean that CRAs, furnishers of information, and users will perform automatically their legal duties. In fact, the entire approach of this book plans for the reality that in some cases, violations will occur because you will not be taken seriously. But now, there's a difference; by following the requirements of the FCRA, you can finally do something about it when violations occur: hire a lawyer to sue them.

* * *

The Law Makes Violators Responsible for Your Damages

Let's cover what the law dictates can happen to those who break the law. First, there are three types of potential violators: the CRAs, furnishers, and users. Let's remind ourselves who are these potential violators. CRAs are consumer reporting agencies; the three big national CRAs are Equifax, Experian and TransUnion. In addition, at least 55 other CRAs operate in this country. Next there are furnishers; these are usually the creditors, debt collectors and gatherers of other information about you that go into the databases of CRAs to be sold to users. Finally, users are those who buy up the data that CRAs package and sell.

The FCRA imposes civil liability upon violators. Two sections of the CRA deal with the civil liability of violators: Sections 1681n, for willful noncompliance, and 1681o, for negligent noncompliance, subject to the limitations set forth in Section 1681h(e). Let's go over each one, with examples.

15 U.S.C. § 1681n - **Civil Liability for Willful Noncompliance**

Any person who willfully fails to comply with the FCRA is liable to the consumer for actual damages, punitive damages as the court may allow, costs of suit, and reasonable attorneys' fees.

Example: Alex Benson is a consumer who noticed that a bankruptcy was on his credit reports. Since Alex had never filed bankruptcy before, he wrote to all three of the CRAs who were reporting this mistake. Forty-five days later, Alex received a letter from each CRA stating that the bankruptcy had been verified. He wrote them again. They wrote back again and stated that the information was verified. Alex hired an attorney and filed suit. He alleged that as a result of the bankruptcy, which did not belong to him, that he had to pay an extra percentage point on his home loan for a 30-year mortgage, which came to $30,000 dollars. During the lawsuit, he deposed the persons most knowledgeable from each CRA, and found out they had not done anything to verify. Alex went to trial and was awarded $30,000 in actual damages, $100,000 in punitive damages, as well as attorneys' fees of $40,000 and costs of $10,000. In addition, his credit reports were finally fixed.

15 U.S.C. § 1681o - **Civil Liability for Negligent Noncompliance**

Any person who negligently fails to comply with the FCRA is liable for actual damages, costs of suit, and reasonable attorney's fees as the court may allow.

Example: Courtney Larson looked at her credit reports and saw that there was a charge off on her AT&T bill showing that the amount was never paid. The debt was reported by ABC debt collectors. In reality, when she received the collection notice, she contacted AT&T, the original debt collector, and paid them the balance owed. She notified the CRAs to conduct an investigation into the matter. The furnisher, ABC, verified the debt without contacting AT&T. Next, Courtney sent the CRAs a copy of the final check (canceled) as proof she had paid it off. The CRA saw the documents and forwarded them to ABC, who took them off the second time after checking with AT&T. Courtney hired an attorney and sued ABC for negligently failing to contact AT&T the first time to confirm payment had been made. Courtney's report was fixed, and she received $5,000 for the pain and anxiety of dealing with this error, plus attorney's fees of $5,000 and costs of $400.

15 U.S.C. § 1681h - **Limitation of Liability**

Money damages that consumers can collect for violations of the FCRA are limited to these two statutes above. For example, you can't sue CRAs or furnishers for defamation or invasion of privacy unless you can prove malicious intent. It's best for most people to hire an attorney to evaluate the estimated value of their case and explore all options before proceeding.

* * *

Hiring a Lawyer

There are so many areas of law in this country, that lawyers must specialize. Think of doctors: some focus on the heart, others on the joints, others on internal organs, etc. It's the same for lawyers. You want to pick a lawyer who, as one of her or his specialties, works in the area of consumer protection on "credit reporting." Overall, consumer protection lawyers are a small bunch nationwide, and even fewer of them practice in the area of credit reporting. You need to find someone who understands this area of the law, someone who is ready and willing to champion your cause.

Our law firm can help you locate qualified attorneys if you have difficulty finding one.

Attorneys' Fees. The statutes cited above, sections 1681n and 1681o, require violators to pay or reimburse your attorneys' fees. Most attorneys will not ask you for any money up front for their fees, but some of them may require you to pay for the costs of filing the lawsuit and other incidental expenses that may be incurred. If you have several attorneys from which to choose, shop around for the best arrangement that suits you. Because attorney's fees are paid by violators, it should not be hard to find one willing to take your case.

On Representing Yourself. Few people are comfortable thinking about representing themselves in court. I would urge you to think twice if you haven't done it before. You must make sure that you have the time and temperament to do it; this is a very technical area of law. The prospect of representing yourself in court is beyond the scope of this book, and I don't recommend it for most of you. Because violators pay attorneys' fees, there is no reason not to consider hiring a competent attorney.

* * *

Settlement v. Trial

By now, you should know that sometimes, when violators don't mend their ways, you must file a lawsuit. When you do, know that you're entitled to damages for your losses, and that you should be able to find an attorney without paying a hefty retainer fee.

The most common question I get from clients is whether their case has to go to trial. The answer is, probably not. When it comes to civil litigation, most cases settle without a trial. With the growing popularity of mediation and settlement conferences before trial, the chances of settling without trial have dramatically increased.

If you insist on collecting every penny you're owed, you'll probably go to trial, but if you're willing to settle for a discounted amount, a case usually settles. In the settlement, I try to include correction of the error.

* * *

Once the suit is filed, depending upon the severity of the

offenses, settlement discussions can begin very quickly. In fact, as soon as your lawsuit is served upon the Defendant, they will often correct the problem immediately. If monetary damages are sought, both sides are able to communicate and be reasonable, then most cases can be settled in four to six months. That's a welcome time frame for those who have struggled for months or years to have credit report mistakes removed from their credit reports. Sometimes, faster results can occur once a suit has been filed and served.

CHAPTER 15: HELPING POWER

In this book, we've covered how you can empower yourself to eliminate credit errors, penalize impermissible users, obtain your *full* consumer file from each CRA, and invoke credit freezes or fraud alerts from CRAs—all using the Fair Credit Reporting Act. You can either learn the law and apply it yourself, or you can retain a lawyer to do it for you.

* * *

As mentioned in Chapter 2, we offer three options to assist you in exercising your rights. Here's a detailed summary of the services and materials offered with each option:

Option One: Free Credit Fix Power Tools. The book you hold in your hands contains the information you need to know to represent yourself in exercising your rights under the FCRA, with step-by-step instructions. However, if you go to the website CreditFixPower.com, you will also receive free Power Tools, including the following:

- The names, addresses, and website addresses of over 50 additional consumer reporting agencies operating in the United States;
- Basic sample dispute letters;
- Answers to frequently asked questions; and
- Updates and newsletters will be emailed or posted on the website, so check back often.

Option Two: The Credit Fix Power Toolbox. In this package, we offer you the entire Power Toolbox. The entire Toolbox is available for an additional fee. To learn more, go to CreditFixPower.com. You will have access to over 50 letter templates prepared or reviewed by this author, and available in Microsoft Word. These pre-formed letters address every facet of the FCRA covered in this book. With a few tweaks and additions, you can start sending out various letters today!

- Instructions how to use the letters;
- Blank letters to CRAs;
- Impermissible purpose letters;
- Non-reportable letters;
- Fraud alert letters;
- Identity theft “block” or “alert” letters;
- Investigative disclosure letters;
- Noncompliance letters;
- Full-file Disclosure letters;
- Dispute letters to CRAs;
- Direct dispute letters to furnishers;
- Adverse action letters;
- False pretenses letters; and
- Combo letters.

In addition to these letters, you will also have access to additional letters and edits to letters that are adjusted or added in the future. You will also receive newsletters emails with new information and updates.

* * *

Option Three: Attorney Power Package. If you don't have time to develop the skills or don't want to write the letters yourself, we'll do it for you. With this program, you hire my law firm to provide personal assistance helping you order your credit reports, analyze your credit reports and send out letters with the precise verbiage tailored for your situation in compliance with the FCRA. We also keep track of all proper dates and deadlines as well as organizing your files for a lawsuit, should one be required.

* * *

MANY PEOPLE either don't have the time, energy or interest to follow all the steps outlined in this book. So, don't feel bad about it if you're one of those—most are, and we understand! That's why we offer the various levels of service. If you would like to take advantage of these additional services, simply go to our website at CreditFixPower.com to either download the free Power Tools, the Power Toolbox, or to sign up for the Attorney Power Package.

* * *

Social Media

You can visit our Credit Fix Power Facebook page at **Facebook.com/creditfixpower**, where we will make periodic posts. You can also follow us on Twitter at **Twitter.com/creditfixpower**.

* * *

In closing, I want to thank you, the reader, for reading this book. I hope you learned everything you hoped to learn about the FCRA and how to exercise your rights. I welcome any feedback you wish to offer. If there are any corrections needed to the text or concerns about the book, please feel free to contact us at info@creditfixpower.com. If you enjoyed the book and don't mind taking a few minutes, we would love to hear from you in the form of a review of this book on Amazon.com or your place of purchase. Thanks again!

BONUS MATERIALS: AN OVERVIEW OF ADDITIONAL CONSUMER PROTECTION LAWS

Over the years, state and federal governments have gradually added to the arsenal of laws that protect citizens and consumers of the United States of America. State and federal lawmakers have seen the need to protect us as society changes and financial institutions and corporate entities consolidate and become stronger and stronger, creating an unequal balance of power and negotiation between individuals and large entities. We refer to these laws collectively as consumer protectionism. It is a movement that will only continue growing.

Some of these other consumer protection laws dovetail with the FCRA. For example, violators of the FCRA often violate the Fair Debt Collection Practices Act (FDCPA). Sometimes violators of the FCRA and FDCPA also violate the Telephone Consumer Protection Act (TCPA)

Other consumer laws besides the FCRA, FDCPA, and TCPA include the Truth in Lending Act: (Visit https://www.law.cornell.edu/uscode/text/15/1601), Repossession Laws, Foreclosure and Loan Servicing Laws, Bankruptcy Laws, Unfair and Deceptive Trade Practices (UDAP) acts, automobile laws (lemon laws, for example), the Fair Credit Billing Act (Visit https://www.law.cornell.edu/uscode/text/15/1666) and Equal Opportunity Employment Laws, to name just a few.

Because FCRA, FDCPA and/or TCPA violations often go hand-in-hand, especially when dealing with debt collectors and debt buyers, I'm going to devote some attention to these laws in this bonus section.

* * *

The Equal Credit Opportunity Act (ECOA)

The Equal Credit Opportunity Protection Act (ECOA) is codified right after the FCRA in the United States Code, 15 U.S.C. § 1691 et seq. It passed in 1974 and additional expansions were added as recently as 2013 to include "sex" and "marital status."

The ECOA makes it unlawful for a creditor to discriminate against any applicant seeking credit based on race, religion, color, national origin, marital status or age.

Violators of this statute face punitive damages of up to $10,000. There are caps on damages in class actions suits.

Discussing the specific provisions of the ECOA is beyond the scope of this book, but it may come into play as it relates to the FCRA.

* * *

The Fair Debt Collection Practices Act (FDCPA)

The Fair Debt Collection Practices Act (FDCPA) is codified as 15 U.S.C. § 1692. Often, violations of the FCRA and FDCPA are interrelated. This is because many of the entities that are misreporting your information to the CRAs are debt collectors. The FDCPA was written to govern the conduct of debt collectors. Often, the misreporting of information to the CRAs and the unlawful collection of debts stems from the same source—the lack of verifiable information about the debt.

Without going into too much detail, here are some common violations that I have seen during my practice in this area. **Remember: you only have one year from the date of a violation in which to file suit against a violator:**

1. A debt collector (DC) is required to write you a letter containing your rights, within 5 days after initial communication (the letter can act as the first contact). See 15 U.S.C. § 1692g(a).

2. You can request validation of the debt within 30 days of the initial written communication. If they don't validate the debt, then they must stop trying to collect until proof is provided. See 15 U.S.C. § 1692g(b).

3. Additional interest cannot be charged on the amount being collected after it has been charged off. See 15 U.S.C. § 1692f(1).

4. A DC may not make false, misleading or deceptive statements or means to collect a debt, including communicating credit information which is known or should be known to be false to anyone (including a CRA). See 15 U.S.C. § 1692e(8).
5. A DC may not make harassing or abusive calls, including repeated calls on the phone with intent to annoy, abuse, or harass the consumer. See 15 U.S.C. § 1692d.
6. A DC may not call before 9 am or after 8 pm. See 15 U.S.C. § 1692c(a)(1).
7. A DC may not call consumers at work if the DC has "reason to know" that your employer prohibits employee from receiving such calls.

* * *

The Telephone Consumer Protection Act

The Telephone Consumer Protection Act is another federal law codified as 47 U.S.C. § 227.

This law essentially states that a caller (often a debt collector) cannot call or text your mobile phone using an automated telephone dialing system *unless* you have given them your express written consent. Under most circumstances, the permission carries over to a debt collector, who has vicarious permission to call the same number that you gave to the creditor. However, you can revoke permission to have them continue to call you, unless the ability to call you is an essential part of the original contract.

* * *

Miscellaneous Federal Consumer Protection Laws

Besides the FCRA, FDCPA and TCPA, there are also other federal consumer protection laws you may or may not have heard of before. Here are three more that may relate to FCRA violations:

1. **Fair Credit Billing Act (FCBA).** 15 U.S.C. § 1601. This law was enacted in 1974, the same year as the ECOA. It is intended to protect consumers from unfair billing by creditors. Most of the statute contains obvious protections, such as prohibiting the billing of goods to a consumer who did not purchase them, reflecting proper balances owed, charging for goods not delivered or damaged, and not delivering goods as described.
2. **Truth in Lending Act (TILA).** aka Regulation or Reg Z, 12 C.F.R. Part 226. This statute is familiar to most; it requires clear disclosure of key lending terms, such as annualized rate of interest, total amount to be paid on the loan, etc.
3. **Health Insurance Portability and Accountability Act (Visit https://www.hhs.gov/hipaa/index.html).** This statute provides protection for consumer health information.

* * *

State Expansion of Consumer Protection Laws

Consumer rights are expected to continue to grow as lawmakers recognize the need for greater protection. Many states have passed their own consumer protection laws. There are four reasons for this.

First, some state lawmakers have determined that federal laws have not gone far enough in protecting consumers.

Second, some states pass better laws when courts interpret the laws in ways that weaken the protections that the states believe the laws were designed to do.

Third, as laws are applied to actual events, they see weaknesses in the wording of the original laws and seek to plug the gaps and holes in the laws.

Finally, laws are passed by states that are sometimes identical to federal law just in case the federal government decides to change or backtrack on consumer protection laws already passed. In these ways, state legislators make sure that consumer laws remain strong and complete.

In summary, some state laws are weaker than their federal law counterparts, while others are as strong or stronger in that they recognize additional rights.

Nevertheless, state laws are not permitted to "water down" or circumvent federal law. In other words, federal laws provide *minimum* protections to consumers. Below are some examples in which state laws add additional protections to consumers and additional penalties for violators.

1. **The Rosenthal Fair Debt Collection Practices Act, California**. A law similar to the FDCPA, enacted in California. It extends fair and decent debt collection practices to *original creditors*, not just debt collectors. See California Civil Code §§ 1788 et seq. Look up the Rosenthal Act.
2. **Mini TCPA, Connecticut**. Federal penalties for robocalls are from $500 to $1,500 per call. Connecticut's TCPA-like law increases the penalties up to $20,000 per violation! Visit

https://www.cga.ct.gov/asp/cgabillstatus/cgabillstatus.asp?selBillType=Bill&bill_num=209&which_year=2014Public Act No. 14-53.

3. **Use of Credit Reports and Credit Scores by Insurers, Florida**. Florida requires insurance companies to notify consumers when credit reports have been requested and used in determining insurability, the setting of premiums, etc. The law also places limits on the sole use of a credit report when making the decision whether to insure someone. To read the Florida statute, go here: https://www.flsenate.gov/Laws/Statutes/2011/626.9741.

These are just three examples of the many types of laws that states have passed that expand upon federal legal protections afforded to consumers.

APPENDIX 1: THE CASE OF MILLSTONE V. O'HANLON REPORTS, INC.

This is a case about a man who bought insurance for his car through his insurance agent. Days later, however, the policy was canceled. Mr. Millstone, who was the policyholder, wanted to know why. A jury award followed, based upon the violations of the FCRA, specifically a violation of 15 U.S.C. § 1681e(b). See 83 F. Supp. 269, 271 (E.D. Mo. 1974).

This case illustrates that what you see in a credit report can differ from what a decision maker sees—in this case, the insurance company—when they obtain a consumer report; it's not just your financial history. Remember, consumer reports can contain "**any** written, oral, or other communication of **any information** by a consumer reporting agency bearing on a consumer's credit worthiness, credit standing, credit capacity, **character, general reputation, personal characteristics, or mode of living**" that could play a factor in your access to credit, insurance or employment." See 15 U.S.C. 1681a(d)(1).

* * *

MEMORANDUM

WANGELIN, District Judge.

This action is before the Court for decision on the merits following the trial to the Court sitting without a jury.

Plaintiff, James C. Millstone (herein Millstone) brought this action alleging violation of 15 U.S.C. § 1681 et seq., commonly known as the "Fair Credit Reporting Act", against the defendant, O'Hanlon Reports, Inc. (herein O'Hanlon). The Court being fully apprised of the premises hereby makes the following findings of fact and conclusions of law.

Findings of Fact

1. This Court has jurisdiction over the subject matter of this suit and the parties hereto pursuant to 15 U.S.C. § 1681p.

2. The plaintiff, James C. Millstone, is an Assistant Managing Editor of the St. Louis Post-Dispatch, a local daily newspaper. He has worked for the Post-Dispatch in various positions since 1958. Prior to his return to the St. Louis area in 1971, he worked in Washington, D. C. as a correspondent for approximately seven years covering various federal agencies, including the White House, and had an FBI clearance to travel with Presidents Johnson and Nixon.

3. The defendant, O'Hanlon Reports, Inc., is a corporation, formerly known as the National Inspection Bureau, Inc., d/b/a O'Hanlon Reports, Inc., operating under the laws of the State of New York and licensed to do business in the State of Missouri as well as most of the States of the Union. It has as its purpose the investigation and collection of information concerning consumers of predominantly real property insurance and automobile insurance.

4. In August of 1971, Millstone and his family moved to St. Louis, Missouri, so that he might take up his duties as news editor for the St. Louis Post-Dispatch. He thereafter contacted his insurance agent, Norman Kastner, and asked Kastner to place auto insurance for him. Kastner placed the policy with Firemen's Fund Insurance Company. The policy took effect on November 15, 1971, and several days later Millstone, in accordance with 15 U.S.C. § 1681d received a notice that a personal investigation would be made in connection with the new policy.

5. On December 20, 1971, Walter McPherson from the Firemen's Fund Insurance Company informed Kastner (and Kastner informed Millstone) that the policy would be cancelled. After assurances from Kastner of Millstone's character and reputation, the insurance company reversed its decision the following day. Millstone voluntarily cancelled the policy.

6. Millstone discovered from McPherson that the cancellation had been brought about because of a consumer credit report which had been made by the defendant, O'Hanlon Reports, Inc.

7. On December 22, 1971, Millstone went to the office of O'Hanlon Reports where he spoke to William O'Connell, the Office Manager. Millstone was told that he was entitled to know what was in his report but that O'Hanlon was entitled to reasonable notice of

ten (10) days before giving the information. When Millstone protested, O'Connell call-the New York Home Office of O'Hanlon and allowed Millstone to speak to a Kenneth Mitchell. Mitchell told Millstone that the information would be available as soon as possible but that he could not give disclosure immediately because the Millstone file was en route from St. Louis to New York through the mails. After Millstone left the office, O'Connell then mailed the file to New York.

8. On December 28, 1971, Millstone received the disclosure of the information in its file from O'Connell at the O'Hanlon offices. O'Connell read the disclosure from a single sheet of paper which had been prepared by David Slayback, the Vice President of O'Hanlon. The disclosure sheet stated in part that:

"The file shows that you are very much disliked by your neighbors at that location [Millstone's Washington residence], and were considered to be a `hippy type'. The file indicates that you participated in many demonstrations in Washington, D. C., and that you also housed out-of-town demonstrators during demonstrations. The file indicates that these demonstrators slept on floors, in the basement and wherever else there was room on your property. The file shows that you were strongly suspected of being a drug user by neighbors but they could not positively substantiate these suspicions. You are shown to have had shoulder length hair and a beard on one occasion while living in Washington, D. C. The file indicates that there were rumors in the neighborhood that you had been evicted by neighbors from three previous residences in Washington, D. C. prior to living at the 48th Street, N. W. location."

This disclosure sheet which Millstone was not allowed to examine was the only item that Millstone was informed of by O'Connell.

9. After protesting virtually all the information contained in the disclosure, Millstone asked O'Connell to explain certain facts contained therein. O'Connell told Millstone that he had no further information and could not answer the questions. He told Millstone that his instructions from the Home Office were only to read the disclosure sheet prepared in New York and to take careful note of any dispute from the customer. At no time was Millstone allowed to look at the actual consumer report file maintained by O'Hanlon upon him, nor were any actual portions of that file read to Millstone at any time by Mr. O'Connell.

10. O'Connell once again called New York and allowed Millstone to speak. David Slayback defended the method and propriety of disclosure to Millstone and neither would nor could explain such matters as the basis and meaning of the statement that Millstone was strongly suspected of being a "drug user".

11. Slayback ordered the Manager of his Silver Springs office, the office which had conducted the original investigation of Millstone, to re-investigate the information. Raymond T. Jonas, the Branch Manager, took approximately three days to complete the re-investigation and then sent his report to the New York office. This re-investigation report contained statements that the Millstone children had "torn up" part of a neighbor's garden and that Mrs. Millstone had used terms such as "pig", and "old hag" to a neighbor and his wife and that she was considered by the neighbors to be a "paranoid", and that Mr. Millstone was considered to be a "hippy type" because he allowed peace demonstrators to stay in his house. Mrs. Millstone was also alleged to have stated that she would allow her children to use drugs.

12. On or about January 12, 1972, O'Connell notified Millstone that the re-investigation was completed and at a meeting between the two read to Millstone both the first and second disclosure

sheets along with a cover letter written by Mr. Slayback to the Firemen's Fund Insurance Company. The thrust of these documents was to correct the previous allegations that Millstone was a "drug user", "hippy type" and the statements about the "peace demonstrators staying at the Millstone residence".

13. On or about January 15, 1972, the Federal Trade Commission, which had received a complaint and request for investigation from Millstone, contacted O'Hanlon, and informed Millstone that the investigation had commenced.

14. In a registered letter dated January 20, 1972, David Slayback informed Millstone of further information contained in the defendant's files, including previously undisclosed criticism of the Millstone children and a statement that Millstone was "utterly lacking in reason and judgment". After Millstone disputed this information in a telephone conversation he received a letter dated February 17, 1972, in which Slayback informed Millstone that the disputed points were not in the new report and thus would not be re-investigated.

15. In each conversation and meeting with O'Hanlon's agents, Millstone requested to see his file but was flatly denied access to it. After O'Connell mailed the file to the New York office of the defendant it remained there.

16. At no time prior to the filing of this lawsuit was Millstone informed of certain critical comments about his wife contained in his file. Millstone first learned of such criticism upon receipt of the answers to plaintiff's interrogatories.

17. From the period of time beginning December 20, 1971 and continuing until the end of February, 1972, the evidence adduced at trial shows that Millstone suffered significant amounts of worry, anxiety and concern over the information which was contained in

O'Hanlon's file about him and to whom that information was being disseminated. The evidence also shows that his family life was disrupted to the extent of lack of sleep and a general upsetting of the household in work routine.

18. O'Hanlon's procedures for making disclosure to Millstone were in conformity with previously planned procedural processes explained to managers of the defendant's branch offices several months prior to the effective date of the Fair Credit Reporting Act. These procedures were contained in a handbook which each manager received and which was introduced into evidence at the trial as plaintiff's exhibit 13 (herein referred to as Manual). The procedures called for in the Manual state in pertinent part:

The important thing is to NEVER check the files in the presence of the consumer . . . (Manual, § 609-610-611, p. 1.).

Prior to the time of your appointment with the consumer, you will have received the Statement of Disclosure from the Home Office. At the time of your appointment, ANY and ALL information you may have relating to the consumer, such as copies of files, copy of your statement, index cards, etc. are to be in your desk drawer, OUT OF SIGHT, of the consumer. You are not to show anything, or acknowledge that you have anything, other than the Statement of Disclosure.

Actual disclosure will be accomplished by reading the Statement of Disclosure to the consumer. The statement is to be read word for word, at your normal reading speed. It is not to be read slowly enough for anyone to copy down word for word, nor is it to be read so fast that the Consumer will not understand what you are saying. Part or all of the Statement of Disclosure may be re-read if the Consumer indicates that he did not understand what you are telling him. The Consumer and/or the person with him may not have a copy of the Statement, nor may they be allowed to read the Statement, or touch it. (emphasis added by capitalization is that contained in the Manual) (Manual, p. 1-2).

19. The original report on Millstone was prepared by Alexander Mayes, an employee of defendant in defendant's Silver Springs office. Mayes contacted four neighbors of the Millstones on the block where they last lived while residing in Washington, D. C.

20. Of the four persons contacted, one refused to speak to Mayes, two others told him that they knew of trouble in the neighborhood but knew nothing first hand and wished not to become involved. All the data recovered in Mayes' report was gleaned from a discussion with one neighbor identified as one McMillan, now deceased. Mayes gathered the data in a period of less than one-half hour. Mayes worked on a commission basis and received approximately one-third of the fee charged by the defendant, which amounted approximately to $1.85 in the Millstone investigation.

21. The time spent by defendant's agents on gathering information for automobile insurance reports is anywhere from ten minutes to one-half hour. The data gathered for real estate insurance transactions may take slightly longer.

22. An investigator for O'Hanlon such as Mayes would average 140 to 160 reports every two weeks.

23. O'Hanlon's Manual concerning the maximum possible accuracy required of such a business organization dealing in consumer reports states that O'Hanlon must: "Adopt procedures to assure maximum possible accuracy of our information on consumers. We must continue to report our facts as we see them be they favorable or adverse, but we must make an additional effort to be sure of those facts." Concerning adverse information, the

Manual goes on to state: "When adverse information is developed, it should be verified by at least one other source to avoid the reporting of any prejudice or inaccurate information." (Manual, § 607, p. 2). There was no evidence produced which showed any attempt to verify the adverse information in Millstone's file.

24. O'Hanlon continues to maintain the procedures described hereinabove and David Slayback described them as reasonable.

25. Procedures for disclosure have been changed by O'Hanlon since December, 1971; a consumer will now have his file read to him on request after the file has been examined by the Home Office. Defendant continues to reserve the option of not disclosing information about others relevant to the consumer and contained in his file. For example, Slayback testified that if a report contained adverse information of a serious nature about a consumer's wife, the Company would not disclose that information to the consumer. The defendant would only disclose such information to its client.

26. Branch managers of defendant were not prepared by O'Hanlon to conduct disclosures and to answer questions concerning files by the consumers.

27. Concerning the disclosure procedures followed in the instant case, Slayback testified that the first disclosure was incomplete, and the reason therefor was his rush to satisfy Millstone's demand for disclosure; in his letter of January 20, 1972, he informed Millstone that the reason for the exclusion was that he had not received the information from his Silver Springs office at the time that he prepared the first disclosure. He stated that Millstone's "utter lack of reasoning and judgment" could be implied from the contents of the first consumer report.

28. The reason that adverse information about Millstone's wife was contained in the consumer report and not disclosed was not

explained in any way.

29. Millstone's character, reputation in the community, working and personal habits, and the character of his reputation and family was dealt with extensively by character witnesses of national and public reputation at the trial. These character witnesses were unstinting in their praise of Mr. Millstone.

Conclusions of Law

These conclusions will be broken into three parts. Counsel for defendant has placed great emphasis in both his pretrial memoranda and his post-trial briefs on the constitutional problems arising out of such a lawsuit concerning infringement of First Amendment freedoms. Accordingly, the constitutional problem will be dealt with first, and the general law provisions relating to 15 U.S.C. § 1681 et seq., along with damages, will be dealt with separately.

I.

Defendant bases his claim of constitutional privilege upon the holdings of *New York Times v. Sullivan*, 376 U.S. 254, 84 S. Ct. 710, 11 L. Ed. 2d 686 (1964), and *Rosenbloom v. Metro Media, Incorporated*, 403 U.S. 29, 91 S. Ct. 1811, 29 L. Ed. 2d 296 (1971). The chief argument of O'Hanlon is that a credit report is constitutionally protected by the First Amendment guarantees of freedom of the press because it is a matter of general or public interest. While the 8th Circuit has not ruled upon whether the aegis of the First Amendment extends to activities such as those of O'Hanlon, four other Circuit Courts of Appeals have ruled on the same or similar question. These four Courts of Appeals have been quite uniform at holding that the activities and publication of retail credit reports are not speech which should be protected under the First Amendment.[*] Any prospective chilling of First Amendment freedoms should be looked at quite carefully by any court. In the present case at bar, it is this Court's opinion that the reports concerning Millstone which were published by O'Hanlon fall within the realm of commercial speech which is not normally within the protections of the First Amendment. A recent Supreme Court case, *Pittsburgh Press Co. v. Human Rel. Comm'n*, 413 U.S. 376, 93 S. Ct. 2553, 37 L. Ed. 2d 669 (1973), has distinguished New York Times v. Sullivan, supra, in the area of commercial speech. The Supreme Court required that for commercial speech to come within the ambits of New York Times that that speech: "communicated information, expressed opinion, recited grievances, protested claimed abuses, and sought financial support on behalf of a movement whose existence and objectives are matters of the highest public interest and concern." 413 U.S. at 385, 93 S. Ct. at 2559. The facts of this case indicate that the credit reports of O'Hanlon concerning Millstone were distributed for commercial purposes and clearly without regard to social concerns or grievances. Thus, it becomes patently obvious that the protections of the First Amendment will not extend to activities such as those of the defendant, and this case is therefore justiciable.

II.

The remainder of this action revolves around the questions of whether or not defendant O'Hanlon is liable under Section 1681n and Section 1681o of this aforecited title. Section 1681n allows the recovery of actual damages, costs and reasonable attorneys fees along with punitive damages for willful non-compliance with the Act in question, and Section 1681o allows actual damages along with costs and attorneys fees for negligent non-compliance with this

Act. The standard of care imposed by the aforecited statutory sections is that:

Whenever a consumer reporting agency prepares a consumer report it shall follow reasonable procedures to assure maximum possible accuracy of the information concerning the individual about whom the report relates. 15 U.S.C. § 1681e(b).

It is clear to this Court as the trier of fact that the defendant was in violation of § 1681e(b), in that its procedures of gathering personal information about consumers, such as Millstone, was only from neighbors from the consumer's residence and that these items were not verified. The evidence also shows that defendant's agent Mayes knowingly included false information in the report which defendant compiled concerning Millstone. In his report agent Mayes refers to a poll of four neighbors, with full knowledge that he spoke only to three neighbors. Also, the report repeatedly asserts that all of the sources were in agreement when Mayes in fact received information from only one source, Mr. McMillan. Considering the prior unblemished record of Millstone and the fact that defendant's own operations Manual concerning such derogatory information states:

"When adverse information is developed, it should be verified by at least one other source to avoid the reporting of any prejudicial or inaccurate information", the actions of O'Hanlon's agent Mayes are so wanton as to be certainly a willful non-compliance with the standard of care imposed by the Act. These actions by defendant's agent Mayes are so heinous and reprehensible as to justify the harsh damages imposed by Section 1681n. Defendant's methods of reporting on consumer's credit backgrounds as shown at trial were so slipshod and slovenly as to not even approach the realm of reasonable standards of care as imposed by the statute. Defendant's reporting methods were so wanton as to be clearly willful noncompliance with the Fair Credit Reporting Act in the eyes of this Court.

Independent of the previously discussed willful violation of the statute is the defendant's violation of § 1681g(a)(1) in that it failed to disclose, and continued until pre-trial discovery forced such disclosure, the nature and substance of all the information contained in its files concerning Millstone. To say that O'Hanlon was parsimonious in its disclosures in this case would be an exercise in understatement. Defendant has stated to the Court that its policy remains not to disclose certain information to consumers which O'Hanlon itself deems appropriate. The previously quoted sections of defendant's operation Manual are ample evidence of plaintiff's attitudes and actions concerning this matter. Millstone was forced to return to defendants' offices on several occasions and each time was able to elicit a little more information from the defendant which concerned him. At no time until this lawsuit was joined and discovery was undertaken did O'Hanlon inform Millstone of the entire amount of information concerning him in O'Hanlon's files. Concerning disclosure to consumers, the legislative history of the statutory sections states:

The House offered the amendment to delete the words `the nature and substance of' in section 609(1). The intent was to permit the consumer to examine all the information in this file except for sources of investigative information, while not giving the consumer the right to physically handle his file. The Senate conferees did not agree to this amendment, contending that the existing language already accomplished this result. The conferees of both Houses intend that this important provision be so interpreted. United States Code, Congressional and Administrative News, p. 4415 (91st Congress, Second Session, 1970).

O'Hanlon was made aware of this intent by Regulations of the

Federal Trade Commission prior to the effective date of this Act. The actions of O'Hanlon in having the file mailed to its New York office, and instructing its employee in St. Louis to tell Millstone that the file was en route to New York and that he could not tell Millstone what was in it when the file was actually in St. Louis are further indications of the willful non-compliance of defendant with this Act. The whole thrust of defendant O'Hanlon's actions was an attempt to withhold from Millstone the information that was rightfully due him under the law. The evidence in the case at bar as a whole is so overwhelming and persuasive as to leave no other conclusion that O'Hanlon was in willful violation of various previously discussed portions of the Fair Credit Reporting Act and should therefore be subject to the liabilities enumerated in Section 1681n.

III.

In regards to damages, the Court further finds that although plaintiff suffered no lost wages nor incurred medical expenses on the account of the injuries therein, he suffered by reason of his mental anguish and had symptoms of sleeplessness and nervousness which were amply testified to, and because of the repeated and numerous times in which plaintiff had to contact O'Hanlon, in many cases having to leave his employment for meetings on account of the defendant's actions as stated above, the plaintiff is entitled to actual damages in the amount of $2,500.00.

Considering the willful non-compliance of O'Hanlon with the requirements of the statute, this Court will assess the sum of $25,000 against defendant O'Hanlon as punitive damages in this action. This Court also finds that the sum of $12,500 will be awarded to plaintiff from defendant for attorneys fees, and the

Court will further order that defendant pay costs in this matter. In consequence, judgment for the plaintiff as stated above will be entered.

NOTES

Grove v. Dun & Bradstreet, Inc., 438 F.2d 433 (3rd Cir., 1971) cert. den., 404 U.S. 898, 92 S. Ct. 204, 30 L. Ed. 2d 175 (1971); *Kansas Elec. Supply Co. v. Dun & Bradstreet, Inc.*, 448 F.2d 647 (10th Cir., 1971), cert. den. 405 U.S. 1026, 92 S. Ct. 1289, 31 L. Ed. 2d 486 (1972); *Oberman v. Dun & Bradstreet, Inc.*, 460 F.2d 1381 (7th Cir., 1972); *Hood v. Dun & Bradstreet, Inc.*, 486 F.2d 25 (5th Cir., 1973), cert. den. 415 U.S. 985, 94 S. Ct. 1580, 39 L. Ed. 2d 882 (1974).

APPENDIX 2: THE STRUGGLE FOR CONSUMER PROTECTION

As corporations and businesses consolidate and grow, scale and scope throughout the United States and internationally, the gap in bargaining power between consumers and these powerful institutions grows wider by the year.

Large corporations are driven to make as much money as possible for their shareholders—their employment and salaries depend upon it. Sometimes they unwisely choose profits over safety, profits over fairness, and profits over following the law. To curb these tendencies, consumer protection laws were born out of necessity.

* * *

Consumer Protection is Born. Attorney Ralph Nader was an early leader in the consumer protection movement. His book, published in 1995, "Unsafe at Any Speed" spotlighted the reluctance of car manufacturers to implement safety features, focusing particularly on the Chevrolet Corvair. Most manufacturers felt that adding safety features, such as seatbelts, would suggest to the public that their cars were not safe, so they resisted making safer cars. The Department of Transportation was formed as a direct result of the impact of Nader's book.

* * *

Profits Over Safety. Citing another example, Ford Motor Company manufactured the Ford Pinto from 1971 to 1980. The Pinto had one problem: it put the gas tank behind the rear axle. My friend had one of these cars; the top of the gas tank was basically the bottom of the trunk. In rear-end accidents, the tank would rupture, and the car would explode. At least 117 lawsuits were brought against Ford, and it was pointed out that despite the lawsuits, Ford chose "profits over safety," concluding that it would cost less to settle lawsuits than it would to stop manufacturing one of its best-sellers. When jurors caught wind of this, they awarded huge sums in punitive damages against Ford, in one case awarding $125 million (later reduced to $3.5 million).

* * *

A Short History of the Credit Reporting Industry and Federal Regulation

Maintaining and sharing information about consumer creditworthiness began in England in the 1820s, when merchants began sharing information about customers. Collecting and sharing information about consumers began in the United States in 1897.

In the late 1950s, computers rapidly replaced the ways creditors made decisions to extend credit to consumers. The Fair Isaac Corporation (FICO) was founded by mathematicians Bill Fair and Earl Isaac in 1956. By 1958, FICO began selling credit-based scores to lenders. By 2013, over 13 billion FICO scores were sold to lenders. Another 10 percent of the market uses other scoring models.

By the late 1960s, the government began regulating a rapidly-computerized banking industry. The Consumer Credit Protection Act was passed in 1968. An amendment to that law, the Fair Credit Reporting Act, was passed in 1970. Significant compromises were made in the bill, before it became law, to accommodate some of the concerns of consumer reporting agencies. The biggest compromise that affects consumers is the change that made it legal for consumer reporting agencies (CRAs) to report false or erroneous information on your credit report—until the consumer complains! Rather, the law only requires the CRAs to correct or delete false, erroneous or unverified information *after* a consumer has made a proper complaint. If you don't do something about mistakes, in most cases—except violations of Section 1681e(b)—they are well within their rights to ignore reported errors.

In 2003, Congress added the Fair and Accurate Credit Transactions Act (FACTA) to the FCRA, and it has now been blended into the statute, which collectively is still called the FCRA. Basically, these provisions add additional protections against identity theft, and help with reporting identity theft, and blocking your credit from unwanted, prying eyes.

Today, three national consumer reporting bureaus have emerged: Experian, Equifax, and Trans Union. All three of these companies have a history of violations of law, collecting sordid information about consumers, and data breaches.

Experian. TRW, an automotive and aerospace company founded in 1901, began a consumer credit information bureau in the early 1960s. This division was renamed Experian when it was sold. Experian eventually became its own separate entity in 1996. Today, it collects information on more than a billion individuals and businesses, and employs 17,000 people, with annual revenues exceeding $4 billion. An Experian subsidiary (Court Ventures) sold personal information to identity thieves, who took the data and offered for sale information on hundreds of thousands of Americans. The information sold included names, dates of birth, social security numbers, driver's licenses, bank account information, passwords, etc. In 2015, Experian revealed a data breach, exposing the sensitive data of 15 million people. The Consumer Financial Protection Bureau fined Experian $3 million in 2017 for deceiving consumers about the use of credit scores it sold to consumers (Experian told consumers their scores were being used by consumers when in fact they were not—they were looking at other data not on these reports). https://www.consumerfinance.gov/about-us/newsroom/cfpb-fines-experian-3-million-deceiving-consumers-marketing-credit-scores/. Experian is sued repeatedly by consumers for violations of the FCRA.

Equifax. This company was founded in Atlanta, Georgia in 1899 as Retail Credit Company. Its primary focus was on selling information to insurance companies. It sold information about a person's "health, habits, morals, and use of vehicles and finances." By the 1960s, it was reported that they collected "facts, statistics, inaccuracies and rumors...about virtually every phase of a person's life: his marital troubles, jobs, school history, childhood, sex life and political activities." See Separating Equifax from Fiction, https://www.wired.com/1995/09/equifax/, Wired, Simson Garfinkel, September 1, 1995. The computerization of this information, leading to wider availability, led to congressional hearings in 1970, and from that, the enactment of the Fair Credit Reporting Act (FCRA), also passed in 1970. Most notably, in September 2017, Equifax announced an unprecedented data breach, exposing the sensitive data of over 145 million U.S. consumers to cybercriminals. Equifax has also been sued repeatedly over the years for violations of the FCRA.

TransUnion. TransUnion began compiling and acquiring credit data in 1968. In 2017, Equifax and TransUnion signed an agreement with the CFPB, agreeing to pay more than $17.6 million in restitution damages to consumers as well as a fine of $5.5 million for deceiving the consumers about the usefulness and cost of credit scores they sold to consumers, as well as luring them into paying for costly credit-related products (such as credit monitoring) with false promises. Visit https://www.consumerfinance.gov/about-us/newsroom/cfpb-orders-transunion-and-equifax-pay-deceiving-consumers-marketing-credit-scores-and-credit-products/. Like the other two CRAs, TransUnion is sued often for violations of the FCRA. In 2017, a California jury awarded class action members $60 million to consumers who TransUnion were falsely reporting to United States government to be terrorists. It's the largest FCRA violation verdict in history.

APPENDIX 3: THE CFPB - A STAR IS BORN

The economic meltdown that began in 2007 was the worst economic downturn since the Great Depression. Out of this financial disaster came one bright spot for consumers. A star was born: the creation of a federal agency known as the Consumer Financial Protection Bureau (CFPB).

Although it went through a questionable and rocky beginning, it has proven to be a powerhouse of protection for consumers. The CFPB is the 800-pound gorilla that oversees consumer complaints and goes after the largest consumer abusers in the United States. The CFPB is leveling the playing field for consumers in an era when increasingly larger institutions have been trampling the rights of consumers with impunity.

The Federal Communications Commission (FCC) and the Federal Trade Commission (FTC) have both turned over some regulatory power to the CFPB, which has taken over or is sharing jointly some of the powers previously exercised by them.

The CFPB was formed out of the passage of federal legislation known as the Dodd-Frank Wall Street Reform and Consumer Protection Act of 2010. Although I personally believe that this act went too far in how much it regulates the banking industry, as far as consumers are concerned, its formation was sorely needed.

The Dodd-Frank Act has given consumer protection a greater voice and clout than ever before. Richard Cordray, the first Director of the CFPB (who was a five-time undefeated champion of Jeopardy!), went right to work, exposing the shady practices of many large corporations, uncovering how they prey upon consumers in ways that consumer law attorneys have fought against for years.

* * *

The CFPB has breathed new life into the consumer protection movement, which had stagnated for years. The CFPB has demonstrated, on a national scale, that consumers needed protection from unscrupulous business practices that took advantage of consumers.

In the eyes of those who have suffered grave injustices at the hands of violators, the CFPB, https://www.consumerfinance.gov/about-us/the-bureau/creatingthebureau/ is a welcome voice and advocate of consumer rights:

"The CFPB consolidates most Federal consumer financial protection authority in one place. The consumer bureau is focused on one goal: watching out for American consumers in the market for consumer financial products and services."

* * *

Here are some of the problems and abuses that the CFPB has exposed since it began operations in mid-2011:

Key Consumer Protection Accomplishments

For nearly six years, the Consumer Financial Protection Bureau (CFPB) has held financial companies accountable and protected consumers from unfair, deceptive, and fraudulent practices, returning billions of dollars to millions of consumers, including students and service members.

Charged with overseeing and enforcing Federal consumer financial protection laws, the CFPB works to ensure that when a consumer uses financial products—credit cards, mortgages, and student loans among others—she or he can make choices based on honest, accurate information about costs and risks.

The CFPB also ensures that financial companies don't take advantage of their customers by establishing and enforcing rules that protect consumers. The CFPB has created stronger consumer financial markets, increased transparency in the marketplace, and has established necessary safeguards against predatory lending practices.

Below are several key accomplishments that have benefited consumers since the Dodd-Frank Wall Street Reform and Consumer Protection Act was enacted:

Securing Almost $12 Billion in Consumer Relief

- The CFPB helped over 29 million individual consumers receive $11.8 billion dollars in due relief, while responding to over 1 million consumer complaints since openings its doors.
- Through enforcement action alone, the CFPB reduced $7.7

billion in consumer debts while winning $3.7 billion in compensation for consumers.

- Nearly 50 million households have benefited from new CFPB mortgage servicing protections that protect consumers from surprise costs and terms when repaying their mortgage, and offer additional protection if a borrower falls behind on their mortgage payment.
- More recently, the CFPB, partnering with the Los Angeles City Attorney's Office and the Office of the Comptroller of the Currency, uncovered deceptive banking practices at Wells Fargo Bank defrauding millions of customers. Enforcement action by the CFPB forced Wells Fargo to pay full refunds to consumers harmed by illegal practices and to pay a $100 million penalty for their wanton behavior. Visit https://www.consumerfinance.gov/about-us/newsroom/consumer-financial-protection-bureau-fines-wells-fargo-100-million-widespread-illegal-practice-secretly-opening-unauthorized-accounts/ to read more. It also fined Wells Fargo $1 billion for auto-loan administration and mortgage practices. Visit https://www.consumerfinance.gov/about-us/newsroom/bureau-consumer-financial-protection-announces-settlement-wells-fargo-auto-loan-administration-and-mortgage-practices/ to read more.

* * *

Protecting Service Members from Predatory Practices

The CFPB's enforcement actions provided $130 million in due compensation to service members, veterans, and their families that were harmed by illegal private sector predatory practices.

In collaboration with the Department of Defense (DOD), the Office of Servicemember Affairs at the CFPB visited more than 145 military installations, handling over 71,000 consumer complaints from service members and their families, and advised DOD on better rules to protect service members from financial exploitation.

* * *

CARD

The Credit Card Accountability, Responsibility and Disclosure Act (CARD), visit https://www.law.cornell.edu/uscode/text/15/1601, now under CFPB jurisdiction, reined in usurious late fees charged on credit cards, limited predatory practices targeting young consumers on college campuses, curtailed sharp interest rate hikes, increased access to consumer credit, and made credit card costs more transparent, saving consumers more than $16 billion in undisclosed fees.

Saving Consumers $16 Billion in Undisclosed Credit Card Fees

- The number of new consumer credit cards increased steadily since the implementation and enforcement of the CARD Act to 6.5 million new credit cards and $37.5 billion in available credit in July of 2016.
- In collaboration with private industry, the CFPB made it easier for stay-at-home spouses to gain access to credit cards by allowing them to use total household income in their applications for new accounts or higher credit limits. This has helped more than 16 million married individuals who do not work outside the home access necessary credit.

These accomplishments of the CFPB come from the following Senate report:

https://www.jec.senate.gov/public/_cache/files/78b1266d-f6c1-4d5b-93ac-62ccb538dfa7/consumer-protection-accomplishments-final-4-10-jw-lv-002-.pdf

APPENDIX 4: STATUTORY CONVERSION TABLE FOR THE FAIR CREDIT REPORTING ACT

The Fair Credit Reporting Act (FCRA) has officially been codified in the United States Code as 15 U.S.C. §1681 et seq. However, many publications, including material published by the federal governing body of the FCRA, the Federal Trade Commission (FTC), still refer to the original codification, which begins from 601 and ends with section 629.

So, for example, 15 U.S.C. § 1681i is the same as "Section 611" or "§ 611." The following table is a complete list of the statutes, so that you may easily identify which section of the law is being referred to, depending upon which codification you are looking at.

FCRA Statute Conversion Table

15 U.S.C. § 1681 et seq and Section 601 et seq

Each of sections is the same as the other:

1681, 602

1681a, 603

1681b, 604

1681c, 605

1681c-1, 605A

1681c-2, 605B

1681d, 606

1681e, 607

1681f, 608

1681g, 609

1681h, 610

1681i, 601

1681j, 612

1681k, 613

1681l, 614

1681m, 615

1681n, 616

1681o, 617

APPENDIX 5: WHERE TO LEARN MORE ABOUT THE FCRA

Like many other laws, the FCRA is not an easy law to understand. If you are committed to understanding the various provisions of the FCRA, you will need to devote considerable time to understanding both the language, the purpose of the law, and how it is interpreted.

In this Appendix, I offer some ways in which you can access the law. I also offer some links to materials that will help you better understand this law as quickly as possible.

1. **Reading the Statute**. The best place that I have found to read the federal statute is to go to the website maintained by Cornell University. The link to their law website is https://www.law.cornell.edu. Visit https://www.law.cornell.edu/uscode/text/15/1681 to start reading the FCRA. This website lays out the statute in a readable format

better than any other website that I have found, other than paid-for services like LexisNexis or Westlaw. Consider donating to their website to keep the content up-to-date and online. Visit https://give.law.cornell.edu/give/106756/#!/donation/checkout to donate. I donate a few bucks every few months, depending upon how often I use it, just as I do for Wikipedia.

2. **Understanding the Statute**. A great place to start understanding the FCRA (besides this book) are resources, (visit https://www.ftc.gov/tips-advice/business-center/privacy-and-security/credit-reporting) from the FTC. Visit (https://www.ftc.gov/tips-advice/business-center/guidance/consumer-reports-what-information-furnishers-need-know) to learn about the duties of furnishers. One of their more helpful links is a discussion about credit freezes and fraud alerts. Visit https://www.ftc.gov/news-events/blogs/business-blog/2017/09/fraud-alerts-vs-credit-freezes-ftc-faqs. The FTC has a lot of good information (https://www.consumer.ftc.gov/articles/0497-credit-freeze-faqs) to navigate this topic.

3. **Summary of Rights**. For a summary of your rights, review this pdf: https://www.consumer.ftc.gov/articles/pdf-0096-fair-credit-reporting-act.pdf. Nolo.com provides another solid overview. For another great overview, visit http://www.creditreporting.com/fair-credit-reporting-act/.

4. **Offline Resources**. There is no better set of books that painstakingly go through the nuances of the FCRA like the two-volume set offered by the National Consumer Law Center. You can order them here: https://library.nclc.org/fcr.

APPENDIX 6: E-OSCAR CREDIT DISPUTE CODES

This is a complete list of all 30 codes identified and used within the e-Oscar notification system:

001: Not his or hers. Provide or confirm complete ID.

002: Belongs to another individual with same/similar name. Provide or confirm complete ID (including Social Security Number, Date of Birth, Generation Code, etc.).

006: Not aware of collection. Provide or confirm complete ID and verify Account Status. Payment Rating, Account History, Original Creditor Name and Creditor Classification.

008: Late due to change of address - never received statement. Verify Account History, Account Status, and Payment Rating.

010: Settlement or partial payments accepted. Verify current Account Status, Payment Rating, Special Comment Code, Account History and Current Balance.

012: Claims Paid the original creditor before collection status or paid before charge-off. Verify Account Status. Payment Rating,

Current Balance, Amount Past Due and Account History, Last Payment Date.

014: Claims paid before collection status.

015: Credit Limit and/or High Credit amount incorrect.

019: Included in the bankruptcy of another person. Verify ECOA Code, Consumer Information Indicator, Account Status, and Current Balance.

023: Claims account closed. Verify Date Closed. Compliance Condition Code and Special Comment Code.

024: Claims account closed by consumer. Verify Compliance Condition Code and Date Closed.

031: Contract cancelled or rescinded. Verify Account Status.

037: Account included in bankruptcy. Verify Consumer Information Indicator, Account Status, Current Balance, Amount Past Due, Payment Rating, and Account History.

038: Claims active military duty. Verify Account Status, Payment Rating, Current Balance, Amount Past Due, Special Comment Code and Account History.

039: Insurance claim delayed. Verify Account History. Account Status. Payment Rating. Amount Past Due and Current Balance.

040: Account involved in litigation. Provide or confirm complete ID and verify all account information.

041: Claims Victims of Natural or Declared Disaster. Verify Account Status, Payment Rating, Special Comment Code, Current Balance, Amount Past Due and Account History.

100: Claims account deferred. Verify Specialized Payment Indicator and Deferred Payment Start Date.

102: Account reaffirmed or not included in bankruptcy. Verify Consumer information indicator, Account Status, Payment Rating, Account History, and Current Balance.

103: Claims true identity fraud/account fraudulently opened. Provided of confirm complete ID.

104: Claims account take-over, fraudulent charges made on account. Verify Account Status, Payment Rating, Account History, Special Comment Code, and Current Balance.

105: Disputes Date of Last Payment/Date of First Delinquency/Date Closed. Verify all dates.

106: Disputes present/previous Account Status/Payment History Profile/Payment Rating. Verify Account History, Account Status, and Payment Rating.

107: Disputes Special Comment/Compliance Condition Code/Narrative Remarks. Verify Special Comment, Compliance Condition Code, and Account Type.

108: Disputes Account Type or Terms Duration/Terms Frequency of Portfolio Type. Verify Account Type, Terms Duration, Terms Frequency and Portfolio Type.

109: Disputes Current Balance, Original Loan Amount, Scheduled Monthly Payment Amount, Actual Payment Amount, Amount Past Due, or Original Charge-off Amount. Verify Original Loan Amount, Scheduled Monthly Payment Amount, Actual Payment Amount, Amount Past Due, Current Balance and Original Charge-off Amount.

110: Claims company will change. Verify all account information.

111: Claims company will delete. Verify all account information.

112: Consumer states inaccurate information. Provide or confirm complete ID and account information.

704: MRC USE ONLY. ATTN: Fraud Department: Item blocked per valid copy of police report received confirming consumer is a victim of fraud.

INDEX

END NOTES

---

[i] https://mashable.com/article/google-location-history-tracking/#u6P.RiNgY5ql

[ii] https://ww.consumerreports.org/privacy/how-facebook-tracks-you-even-when-youre-not-on-facebook/

[iii] https://www.washingtonpost.com/apps/g/page/world/how-the-nsa-is-tracking-people-right-now/634/?noredirect=on;%20https://en.wikipedia.org/wiki/PRISM_(surveillance_program)

[iv] http://www.spiegel.de/international/world/privacy-scandal-nsa-can-spy-on-smart-phone-data-a-920971.html

Made in the USA
Monee, IL
04 November 2026

67378011R00085